Fido's Finest

Traveling With Your Pet...In Style

Colorado Edition

www.fidosfinest.com

ISBN: 0-9768821-0-8 Paperback

This book is printed on acid free paper.

About the Author

Bridgette (Bellamy) Maxwell was born in 1970, the year of the dog! Naturally, she comes from a long line of animal lovers. "We always had dogs when I was growing up, and they were part of the family."

In 1992, she moved from Michigan City, Indiana to Crested Butte, Colorado (aka: A Pooch's Paradise). In 1994, also the year of the dog, she could no longer hold back and adopted then seven week old Shamus from a western slope Humane Society. "My life then changed forever...and for the better." Living in a mountain / ski town with "off seasons", free time became plentiful, and they found themselves on road trips nearly three months of the year. Her love for Shamus' constant companionship and traveling have once again come together, creating the second edition of Fido's Finest!

Acknowledgements

Thanks to my family and friends who have been so incredibly supportive of this project. Special thanks to: Mom and Dad, of course. Thanks also to my wonderful in-laws. I appreciate my supportive friends; Jensta, Melissa, Kelly, Waddles, Laurel, Sarah, Cindy, Le Anne and Laura.

Extra thanks to:

Thanks to Bob Henry (the man) once again for the layout/design & hard work and thank you to Lisa Sacco & Scout for their great work.

Thanks to Zachary Reece, once again for the cover design. Thank You to all of the businesses, hotel managers and employees listed in the book and of course... anyone I so rudely forgot! Thanks Shamus, for putting up with all the hotel hopping again! Most of all, thank you for your vast patience, confidence and support, my amazing husband and soul mate, Brandon!

Cover Illustration by Zachary Reece.

Back cover photo by Brandon Maxwell.

Book design/layout, editing, cover layout, and internal ad design by Blue Sky Creative Services.

This travel guide is intended to provide useful information to those who travel with their pets. The ratings are based on vast experience, but also on opinion. Please note that change of information or pet policies is inevitable. The Author of Fido's Finest claims no responsibility for any changes, errors or properties which do not meet expectations. I apologize for any inconvenience. Contact properties in advance to confirm current policies.

A Few Words About Petiquette

There are so many great places to stay with your pet throughout Colorado. Most of these hotels realize the caliber of guests who travel with their pets. If everyone does their share by following the rules, then everyone can continue to enjoy these fantastic properties as pet friendly lodging options. So, please be considerate and respect each property's pet policy.

If your dog is a constant barker or a furniture chewer, your dog is not travel friendly. Chances are, he would probably prefer being on his own turf with a pet sitter.

When staying in hotels, please be aware of your pet's actions at all times. Always keep your pet on a leash unless you are in the privacy of your hotel room. Not everyone is an animal lover (boy are they missing out) and some people are highly allergic, so pay attention to your pet getting in other people's space. If you are waiting for the elevator and someone looks uncomfortable with your dog, wait for the next elevator.

Many of our pets are used to laying on the couch, the bed or maybe a favorite chair. Can you blame them? Breaking them of this habit while in a hotel room can sometimes be difficult, if not impossible. It's a good idea to carry a sheet or blanket with you to cover and protect the pooch's "chosen place to lounge". Pet hair can be difficult to remove from many fabrics, so do your share and be aware. Buy a disposable, sticky lint brush. If your pet gets on the unprotected bed or furniture in the hotel, simply roll the brush and it instantly picks up pet hair. You will also be increasing the odds of getting your deposit back if this applies. Many hotels require a housekeeping inspection before they dismiss the damage deposit on your credit card.

Inspiration!

My dog Shamus, a Labrador / Dingo mix and Colorado native, has been the inspiration behind Fido's Finest. We have driven from Seattle to Key West, San Diego to Maine and about everywhere in between, seeking out the finest pet friendly accommodations available. Of course, our home state of Colorado is our specialty! Shamus has dictated the most amazing vacations. We would have never discovered so many hidden treasures if it weren't for him. While strutting through several luxurious hotel lobbies, Shamus has shocked so many envious pet owners who were unaware of the pet friendly policies. We decided it was time to share our coveted information with our fellow pet lovers. Within the contents of this book, you will find over 240 of the best pet friendly accommodations we have discovered in every part of Colorado.

From Alamosa to Yampa, this user-friendly travel guide lists valuable lodging information for those who travel with their pets. Don't leave home without 'em!

— Bridgette

—Fido's Finest is dedicated to my one and only Shamus!–

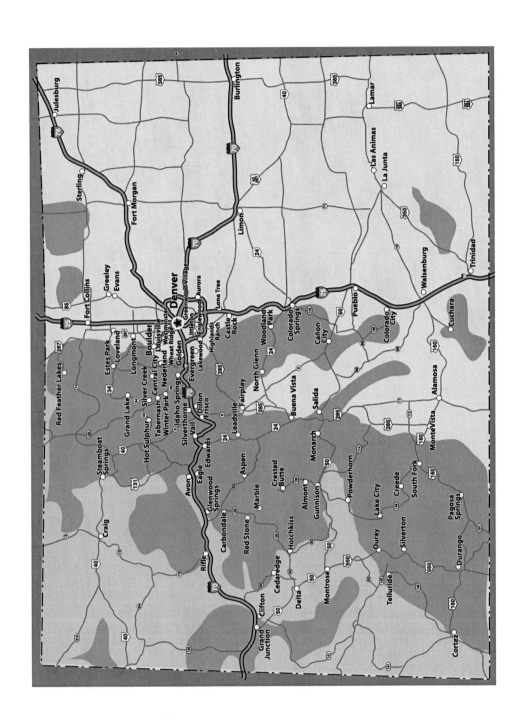

Ratings-

One Paw Status: 🐾
Clean, Safe and Comfortable Accommodations.

Two Paw Status: 🐾 🐾
A notch above the one paw with an extra amenity or two.

Three Paw Status: 🐾 🐾 🐾
A high quality property with several extra amenities.

Four Paw Status: 🐾 🐾 🐾 🐾
An outstanding property with many extra luxurious comforts, services and amenities.

Five Paw Status: 🐾 🐾 🐾 🐾 🐾
A fine hotel earns this title by really taking the extra step, making sure both you and your pet have a remarkable experience.

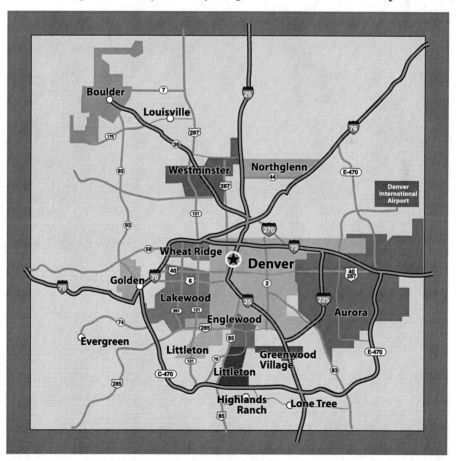

-Alamosa-

Best Western Alamosa Inn
2005 Main Street 81101
719-589-2567 / 800-459-5123

Restaurant: Walking distance

H20: Indoor pool and hot tub

Pet Fee: $10 per stay per pet

Refundable Pet Deposit: None

Size Limit: None

Terms: Well-behaved pets welcome.

Pet Amenities: Pet pick up bags are available at the front desk. There are grassy areas to walk your dogs on property.

Clarion Hotel of The Rio Grande
333 Santa Fe Avenue 81101
719-589-5833 / 800-669-1658

Restaurant: Clancy's

H20: Indoor pool and hot tub

Pet Fee: None

Refundable Pet Deposit: $25

Size Limit: None

Terms: Must declare pets at check in.

Pet Amenities: Grassy area on south side of building for walking dogs.

Days Inn
224 O'Keefe Drive 81101
719-589-9037 / 800-DAYS-INN

Restaurant: Two within walking distance.

H20: None

Pet Fee: $10 per day per room

Refundable Pet Deposit: None

Size Limit: Prefer smaller dogs. Call in advance for availability.

Terms: Well-behaved pets are welcome.

Pet Amenities: Grassy park nearby for walking pets.

Traveling With Your Pet ...In Style!

-Almont-

Almont Resort
10209 Highway 135 81210
970-641-4009

Restaurant: Almont Resort Restaurant

H20: None

Pet Fee: $10 per day per pet

Refundable Pet Deposit: None

Size Limit: None

Terms: Guest is responsible for damage caused by pets.

Pet Amenities: Three rivers for your dogs to swim, hiking trails nearby.

Three Rivers Resort
130 County Road 742 81210
970-641-1303 / 888-761-3474

Restaurant: Walking distance

H20: None

Pet Fee: $15 per stay per pet

Refundable Pet Deposit: None

Size Limit: None

Terms: Guest is responsible for damage. Pets cannot be left in cabins unattended. Well-behaved pets welcome.

Pet Amenities: Three convenient rivers for your dog's swimming pleasure.

-Aspen-

Aspen Meadows Resort
A Dolce Conference Destination
845 Meadows Road 81611
970-925-4240 / 800-452-4240

Restaurant: The Restaurant at The Aspen Meadows, Plato's View on the upper deck.

H20: Year round outdoor heated pool and hot tub.

Pet Fee: None

Refundable Pet Deposit: $100

Size Limit: None

Terms: Pets cannot be left in room unattended.

Pet Amenities: 40 acre property with plenty of grassy areas to walk pets. Pet pickup stations around property.

Aspen Mountain Lodge

311 West Main Street 81611

970-925-7650 / 800-362-7736

Restaurant: Several within walking distance.

H20: Year round outdoor pool and hot tub.

Pet Fee: $20 per pet per night

Refundable Pet Deposit: None

Size Limit: None

Terms: Well-behaved pets are welcome. If pet is left alone in room, the staff requests a contact phone number.

Pet Amenities: There is a park a few blocks away to walk your pets. Treats at check in.

The Brand Building

205 South Galena Street 81611

970-920-1800

Restaurant: Several within walking distance

H20: None

Pet Fee: None

Refundable Pet Deposit: None

Size Limit: None

Terms: Must be a nice, happy dog.

Pet Amenities: Doggie Bowls. The staff welcomes special requests.

Fido's Favorite Features: Luxurious accommodations, fine bedding, ideal downtown location. There are six apartment style rentals, all tastefully decorated, each with their own style.

"A dog has the soul of a philosopher."

-Plato

Hotel Aspen

110 West Main Street 81611

970-925-3441 / 800-527-7369

> **Restaurant**: Walking distance
>
> **H20**: Outdoor pool and 2 hot tubs.
>
> **Pet Fee**: $20 per night per room, not to exceed $60 for entire stay.
>
> **Refundable Pet Deposit**: None
>
> **Size Limit**: Large pets discouraged. No cats allowed.
>
> **Terms**: Pets rooms are on the first floor.
>
> **Pet Amenities**: Pet pick up bags and treats at check in. There are several parks within walking distance.

Hotel Jerome

330 East Main Street 81611

970-920-1000 / 800-331-7213

> **Restaurant**: Jacob's Corner, Century Room, J Bar, The Library
>
> **H20**: Outdoor pool and two hot tubs.
>
> **Pet Fee**: $75 per room per stay
>
> **Refundable Pet Deposit**: None
>
> **Size Limit**: None
>
> **Terms**: Guest accepts responsibility for pet's behavior.
>
> **Pet Amenities**: "J Bones", logo stamped and made in house accompany a personalized welcome letter for each pet guest. Pet sitting and dog walking are available. Pet wellness center nearby.
>
> **Fido's Favorite Features**: Great location, tasteful decor, wonderful bath products. This is a very impressive property which definitely welcomes pets.
>
> * Outside the front door of the magnificent Hotel Jerome, it's only a short walk to The Rocky Mountain Pet Shop. They carry healthy foods, yummy treats and a variety of supplies for your pet.

If your dog gets "skunked", soak him with tomato juice before bathing him thoroughly.

Hotel Lenado

200 South Aspen Street 81611

970-925-6246 / 800-321-3457

Restaurant: Markham's

H20: Outdoor hot tub

Pet Fee: None

Refundable Pet Deposit: None

Size Limit: None

Terms: Guest must request a pet room when booking reservation due to limited amount of pet rooms. Pets must exit through outside guest doors.

Pet Amenities: Bass Park is located behind the hotel.

Fido's Favorite Features: This small hotel's included gourmet breakfast is fantastic.

Limelite Lodge & The Snowflake Inn

228 East Cooper Avenue 81611

970-925-3025 / 800-433-0832

Restaurant: Walking distance

H20: Three outdoor pools and three hot tubs

Pet Fee: $10 per pet per night

Refundable Pet Deposit: None

Size Limit: None

Terms: Pets cannot be left in room unattended.

Pet Amenities: Wagner Park is located next to the lodge.

The Journey Begins

The Sky Hotel welcomes all adventure seeking dogs and their owners who think they can keep up.

- The Dog's Life Package

The Sky Hotel, Aspen Colorado 800-882-2582

CB PAWS

The Little Nell 🐾 🐾 🐾 🐾 🐾

675 East Durant Avenue 81611

970-920-4600 / 888-843-6355

> **Restaurant**: Montagna, Greenhouse Bar
>
> **H20**: Outdoor pool and hot tub
>
> **Pet Fee**: None
>
> **Refundable Pet Deposit**: None
>
> **Size Limit**: None
>
> **Terms**: Guest is responsible for any damage caused by pets. Dog biscuits upon check in. Hiking trails nearby.
>
> **Fido's Favorite Features**: Top notch rooms, superior bedding, wonderful bath products, prime location. Conveniently located just steps from the Silver Queen gondola, which allows pets during the summer months. If you have high standards, The Little Nell is second to none.

The Residence Hotel 🐾 🐾 🐾 🐾 🐾

305 South Galena Street 81611

970-920-6532

> **Restaurant**: Walking distance
>
> **H20**: None
>
> **Pet Fee**: None
>
> **Refundable Pet Deposit**: None
>
> **Size Limit**: None
>
> **Terms**: There will be a professional cleaning fee for any room left with an exceeding amount of pet hair, odor or mess caused by pets.
>
> **Pet Amenities**: Max the dog, is the General Manager who will greet you and your pet. The hotel will gladly watch over your pet while you are out and they can also make grooming arrangements for you.
>
> **Fido's Favorite Features**: One of a kind suites with beautifully elegant decor. Excellent downtown location. This unique property is sure to please. Very pet friendly staff.
>
> * Max will be happy to lead you and your dog right around the corner to his favorite local store, CB Paws. While visiting Aspen, be sure not to miss this impressive pet boutique. Local dogs know best!

The St. Regis Aspen
315 East Dean Street 81611
970-920-3300 / 888-454-9005

> **Restaurant**: Olives, Shadow Mountain Lounge
>
> **H20**: Outdoor pool and three hot tubs
>
> **Pet Fee**: $100 per stay per pet
>
> **Refundable Pet Deposit**: None
>
> **Size Limit**: None
>
> **Terms**: Well-behaved pets welcome.
>
> **Pet Amenities**: Pet sitting / walking services available. Wagner Park is across the street to walk your pet.
>
> **Fido's Favorite Features**: Olives, wonderful bedding, gorgeous lobby. This fine hotel definitely aims to please.

Sky Hotel
709 East Durant Avenue 81611
970-925-6760 / 800-882-2582

> **Restaurant**: 39 Degrees Lounge
>
> **H20**: Outdoor pool and hot tub
>
> **Pet Fee**: None
>
> **Refundable Pet Deposit**: None
>
> **Size Limit**: None
>
> **Terms**: Owner is responsible for any damage caused by pet.
>
> **Pet Amenities**: For $35 you get a pet amenity bag. There are plenty of areas to walk your pets near property.
>
> **Fido's Favorite Features**: Fantastic location, wonderful outdoor pool area, stylish accommodations. This posh hotel is a short walk from many impressive restaurants and shops.

-Aspen / Snowmass-

Silvertree Hotel
100 Elbert Lane 81615
970-923-3520 / 800-525-9402

Restaurant: Brothers Grille

H20: Outdoor pool and hot tub

Pet Fee: None

Refundable Pet Deposit: None

Size Limit: None

Terms: Well-behaved pets welcome. Must sign pet policy agreement upon check in.

Pet Amenities: Room service menu for dogs and cats. There is an ample pet walking area near the property.

Fido's Favorite Features: Great pool area, excellent location to ski & stay, comfortable accommodations.

Snowmass Mountain Chalet
115 Daly Lane 81615
970-923-3900 / 800-843-1579

Restaurant: Within walking distance.

H20: Year round outdoor pool and hot tub.

Pet Fee: $20 per day per room in the winter, $10 in the summer.

Refundable Pet Deposit: None

Size Limit: None

Terms: Well-behaved pets welcome. Barkers cannot be left in room unattended.

Pet Amenities: Grassy areas to walk pet nearby.

Don't forget to protect your pet against heartworms. Always have your pet tested before starting him on heartworm prevention medication.

Wildwood Lodge
40 Elbert Lane 81615
970-923-3550 / 800-445-1642

> **Restaurant**: Village Steakhouse
>
> **H20**: Outdoor pool and hot tub
>
> **Pet Fee**: None
>
> **Refundable Pet Deposit**: None
>
> **Size Limit**: None
>
> **Terms**: Well-behaved pets welcome. Must sign pet policy agreement upon check in.
>
> **Pet Amenities**: Room service menu for dogs and cats. There is an ample pet walking area near the property.

-Aurora-

Amerisuites - Denver International Airport
16250 East 40th Avenue 80011
303-371-0700 / 800-833-1516

> **Restaurant**: Walking distance
>
> **H20**: Indoor pool
>
> **Pet Fee**: None
>
> **Refundable Pet Deposit**: None
>
> **Size Limit**: None
>
> **Terms**: Responsible for damage. Well-behaved pets are welcome.
>
> **Pet Amenities**: There are areas on property where you can walk your pets.

Best Western Gateway Inn & Suites
800 South Abilene Street 80012
720-748-4800 / 800-WESTERN

> **Restaurant**: Several within walking distance.
>
> **H20**: Indoor pool and hot tub.
>
> **Pet Fee**: $15 per pet per room
>
> **Refundable Pet Deposit**: None
>
> **Size Limit**: None
>
> **Terms**: Well-behaved pets welcome.
>
> **Pet Amenities**: There are grassy areas nearby to walk your pets.

Comfort Inn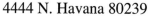
14071 East Iliff Avenue 80014
303-755-8000 / 800-221-2222
Restaurant: Several within walking distance.
H20: None
Pet Fee: $20 per stay per room.
Refundable Pet Deposit: None
Size Limit: 40 lbs.
Terms: Pets cannot be left alone in room.
Pet Amenities: There are grassy areas nearby to walk your pet.

Embassy Suites
Denver International Airport
4444 N. Havana 80239

303-375-0400 / 800-EMBASSY
Restaurant: Giattis
H20: Indoor pool and hot tub
Pet Fee: None
Refundable Pet Deposit: $50 only if paying cash.
Size Limit: None
Terms: Pet must be crated for housekeeping to enter room.
Pet Amenities: Dog treats at check in. Grassy areas to walk pets on properties.
Fido's Favorite Features: Great airport lodging location, Giattis, pet-friendly staff.

Holiday Inn Denver International Airport
15500 East 40th Avenue 80239
303-371-9494 / 800-HOLIDAY
Restaurant: Coffee Terrace
H20: Indoor pool and hot tub
Pet Fee: $25 per stay per room
Refundable Pet Deposit: None
Size Limit: None
Terms: Pets cannot be left unattended in room unless crated.
Pet Amenities: Grassy areas for walking pets

Homestead Studio Suites Hotel Denver/Aurora
13941 East Harvard Avenue 80014
303-750-9116 / 800-EXT-STAY

Restaurant: Several within walking distance.

H20: None

Pet Fee: $25 per day per room, $75 maximum per stay

Refundable Pet Deposit: None

Size Limit: None

Terms: None

Pet Amenities: There are areas to walk your pet on property.

La Quinta Inn
1011 S. Abilene Street 80012
303-337-0206 / 800-531-5900

Restaurant: Walking distance

H20: Seasonal outdoor pool

Pet Fee: None

Refundable Pet Deposit: None

Size Limit: None

Terms: Pets must be removed for housekeeping to enter room.

Pet Amenities: Pet walk area is on the west side of the building.

Sleep Inn Denver International Airport
15900 East 40th Avenue 80011
303-373-1616 / 800 4-CHOICE

Restaurant: Walking distance

H20: Indoor pool

Pet Fee: $10 per pet per day

Refundable Pet Deposit: None

Size Limit: None

Terms: Pets cannot be left in room unattended.

Pet Amenities: There is plenty of space to walk your pet.

"My dog's not spoiled...I'm just well trained!"
-Unknown

-Avon-

Comfort Inn Vail/Beaver Creek

161 West Beaver Creek Blvd. 81620

970-949-5511 / 800-4-CHOICE

Restaurant: Walking distance

H20: Year round outdoor pool and hot tub

Pet Fee: $25 fee per room per stay

Refundable Pet Deposit:

Size Limit: 40 lbs.

Terms: Pets cannot be left in room unattended.

Pet Amenities: Grassy areas on property to walk your pets.

Photo by: Jack Affleck

A pet lover who is

Experienced ~ Knowledgeable ~ Trustworthy

Contact **TOM VUCICH,** Broker Associate
For all your real estate needs in the Vail Valley

Located in the pet-friendly Ritz-Carlton®, Bachelor Gulch
Post Office Box 2820, Avon, Colorado 81620
Toll Free: (888) 677-8380, ext. 2301   Direct: (970) 845-2301
Email: tvucich@slifer.net

SLIFER SMITH & FRAMPTON REAL ESTATE

www.VailFineProperties.com
"Your source for all properties in the Vail Valley"

THE MOST TRUSTED NAME IN **VAIL VALLEY** REAL ESTATE FOR MORE THAN **40** YEARS

THE RITZ-CARLTON, BACHELOR GULCH

THE RITZ-CARLTON, BACHELOR GULCH

The grand lodge architectural style of The Ritz-Carlton, Bachelor Gulch exudes authentic Rocky Mountain luxury and captures the essence of the surrounding national forest. This year-round destination resort offers limitless outdoor activities including unmatched ski-in ski-out access on Beaver Creek Mountain, Colorado's highest rated golfing with preferred tee times at the private Red Sky Golf Club on their two new 18-hole championship courses and the unrivaled luxury of The Bachelor Gulch Spa. The only spa in Colorado to win the coveted Mobil Four-Stars, The Bachelor Gulch Spa at The Ritz-Carlton is a 21,000 square-foot spa and fitness center featuring 19 treatment rooms, a co-ed rock-lined grotto with lazy river hot tub, and both Pilates and yoga studios. It is a relaxing place to rejuvenate after an active or leisurely day on the mountain. Remington's, the resort's signature restaurant features wild game specialties and innovative regional cuisine. Bachelor, the resort's resident Labrador Retriever is available for hikes in Bachelor Gulch through the Loan-a-Lab program and is the perfect activity for the entire family.

BACHELOR AND THE LOAN-A-LAB PROGRAM

The Ritz-Carlton, Bachelor Gulch on Beaver Creek Mountain is quite possibly the most dog-friendly resort in North America. The resort invites guests to bring their dogs to the hotel, but if guests can't, they say, "We'll loan you ours." A hike or winter walk in the snow wouldn't be complete without man's best friend! Bachelor, the resident yellow Labrador Retriever at The Ritz-Carlton, Bachelor Gulch is happy to accompany you and your family on hikes and snowshoe trails throughout Bachelor Gulch. When not out on Beaver Creek Mountain, Bachelor may be found strolling the grounds or laying on his dog bed, known as "The Bachelor Pad" in the Great Room next to the fireplace.

The Loan-a-Lab hiking program is available by reservation through the resort's Concierge. He is available Monday through Friday at 9:00 a.m. and Wednesday and Friday at 1:00 p.m. Children under 16 years of age must be accompanied by an adult. You also can meet Bachelor in the lobby between 1:00 p.m and 3:00 p.m. five days a week. The Loan-a-Lab program is complimentary to resort guests, and a voluntary donation in Bachelor's name may be made to the Eagle Valley Humane Society upon request.

The Ritz-Carlton, Bachelor Gulch, 0130 Daybreak Ridge, P.O. Box 9190, Avon, CO, 81620
Phone: (970) 748-6200 FAX: (970) 343-1070

The Ritz-Carlton Bachelor Gulch

0130 Daybreak Ridge 81620
970-748-6200 / 800-576-5582

>**Restaurant**: Remington's, The Daybreak Deli, The Buffalo Bar
>
>**H20**: Year round outdoor pool and three hot tubs, two indoor hot tubs
>
>**Pet Fee**: $35 per stay per room
>
>**Refundable Pet Deposit**: None
>
>**Size Limit:** None
>
>**Terms**: Dogs only. Guest is responsible for pet's behavior. Must make arrangements with housekeeping if pet is left alone in room.
>
>**Pet Amenities**: Bachelor, the fabulous house dog welcomes you! Pet bed, bowls and treats at check in. There is plenty of room to walk your dogs on and near property. Pet sitting available upon request. The staff welcomes any other special requests.
>
>**Fido's Favorite Features**: The Spa, fabulous accommodations, great location for skiing, Fantastic pool area, The Remington. The Ritz-Carlton Bachelor Gulch is a destination resort which truly has it all.

-Boulder-

Best Western Boulder Inn

770 28th Street 80303
303-449-3800 / 800-233-8469

>**Restaurant**: Fatty J's, The Green Room
>
>**H20**: Indoor hot tub and seasonal outdoor pool
>
>**Pet Fee**: None
>
>**Refundable Pet Deposit**: $100
>
>**Size Limit**: None
>
>**Terms**: Must be on the first floor and in a smoking room. Guest cannot leave pet unattended in room.
>
>**Pet Amenities**: There is a large field across the street from the property where you can walk your pets.

"Scratch a dog and you'll find a permanent job."
-Franklin P. Jones

Boulder Homewood Suites by Hilton

4950 Baseline Road 80303

303-499-9922 / 800-225-5466

> **Restaurant**: Walking distance
>
> **H20**: Seasonal outdoor pool and hot tub
>
> **Pet Fee**: $50 per stay per room
>
> **Refundable Pet Deposit**: None
>
> **Size Limit**: None
>
> **Terms**: Arrange cleaning with housekeeping so pet can be removed.
>
> **Pet Amenities**: Ample walking areas on property, pet welcome basket.
>
> **Fido's Favorite Features**: The impressive expanded continental breakfast and evening Manager's Reception is offered Monday through Thursday. Very pet-friendly staff.

Boulder Outlook Hotel and Suites

800 28th Street 80303

303-443-3322 / 800-542-0304

> **Restaurant**: The Buffalo Sports Bar & Grill
>
> **H20**: Indoor pool and hot tub
>
> **Pet Fee**: None
>
> **Refundable Pet Deposit**: None
>
> **Size Limit**: None
>
> **Terms**: Well-behaved pets welcome.
>
> **Pet Amenities**: Crates available upon request. Outside dog run, guest pet gift upon check in. House calls are available through a local Veterinarian.
>
> **Fido's Favorite Features**: This new eco-friendly hotel chain is a newly remodeled property well worth checking out. The indoor climbing wall is a unique and fun feature.
>
> *Take your dogs to PC's Pantry for a fantastic selection of fresh baked goods, which are meant just for Fido.

Traveling With Your Pet ...In Style!

Boulder University Inn
1632 Broadway 80302
303-417-1700

Restaurant: Within walking distance to several restaurants.

H20: Seasonal outdoor pool

Pet Fee: $15 per day per room

Refundable Pet Deposit: $50

Size Limit: Call in advance

Terms: Well-behaved pets welcome.

Pet Amenities: Walking trail located behind property.

The Boulder Broker Inn
555 30th Street 80303
303-444-3330 / 800-338-5407

Restaurant: Bentley's Lounge, The Broker Restaurant

H20: Outdoor hot tub and seasonal outdoor pool.

Pet Fee: $10 per room per stay

Refundable Pet Deposit: None

Size Limit: None

Terms: Pets cannot be left unattended in room. Guest must sign a pet policy agreement upon check in. Pet rooms are on the first floor only.

Pet Amenities: Ample walking area on the southeast side of building. Boulder Creek Path is also nearby.

Foot of the Mountain Motel
200 Arapahoe Avenue 80302
303-442-5688 / 866-773-5489

> **Restaurant**: Short drive to restaurants.
>
> **H20**: None
>
> **Pet Fee**: $5 per day per room
>
> **Refundable Pet Deposit**: $50
>
> **Size Limit**: None
>
> **Terms**: Pets cannot be left unattended in room.
>
> **Pet Amenities**: Located near the Boulder Creek Trail. Nice park nearby to walk your pets.

Millennium Harvest House Boulder
1345 28th Street 80302
303-443-3850 / 866-866-8086

> **Restaurant**: Thyme on the Creek
>
> **H20**: Seasonal outdoor pool and hot tub, indoor pool and hot tub. (outdoor portion of pool is seasonal)
>
> **Pet Fee**: $25 per day per pet
>
> **Refundable Pet Deposit**: None
>
> **Size Limit**: 100 lbs.
>
> **Terms**: Pet rooms are on the first floor only.
>
> **Pet Amenities**: Boulder Creek Path is located behind the property. There is plenty of room behind the property to exercise your dogs.
>
> **Fido's Favorite Features**: Comfortable accommodations, nice pool area and convenient location. This full service hotel welcomes pets.
>
> * Be sure to take your pooch to Colorado Canines for the latest in healthy treats, foods and other great items to spoil him. A local favorite!

Traveling With Your Pet ...In Style!

Quality Inn & Suites Boulder Creek
2020 Arapahoe Avenue 80302
303-449-7550 / 800-228-5151

> **Restaurant**: Short drive to several restaurants.
>
> **H20**: Indoor pool and hot tub
>
> **Pet Fee**: $15 per night per room.
>
> **Refundable Pet Deposit**: $100
>
> **Size Limit**: None
>
> **Terms**: Pets cannot be left unattended in rooms.
>
> **Pet Amenities**: Dog run on property.

Residence Inn Boulder
3030 Center Green Drive 80301
303-449-5545 / 800-331-3131

> **Restaurant**: Walking distance
>
> **H20**: Outdoor hot tub, seasonal outdoor pool
>
> **Pet Fee**: $50 for 1-10 days, $5 per day after that
>
> **Refundable Pet Deposit**: None
>
> **Size Limit**: None
>
> **Terms**: Must make arrangements with housekeeping to have room cleaned. Must sign the pet policy agreement upon check in.
>
> **Pet Amenities**: Dog bowl with treats upon request. "Pet in Room" magnet for outside of suite door.

-Breckenridge-

Breckenridge Mountain Lodge
600 South Ridge Street 80424
970-547-5725 / 800-832-4025

> **Restaurant**: Breckenridge Brewery is within walking distance
>
> **H20**: Year round outdoor hot tub
>
> **Pet Fee**: $30 per night per room
>
> **Refundable Pet Deposit**: $150
>
> **Size Limit**: None
>
> **Terms**: Adult dogs only. Dogs must be leashed at all times. Pets may not be left unattended in rooms. Owners must pick up after their pets, pick up bags are available. Advance reservations required.
>
> **Pet Amenities**: Doggie dishes and a dog blanket are provided. Plenty of grassy areas to walk your pet.

Great Divide Lodge
550 Village Road 80424
970-547-5725 / 800-832-4025

> **Restaurant**: Breck's Lounge & Restaurant. Room service is also available.
>
> **H20**: Year round indoor and outdoor pool, indoor and outdoor hot tubs.
>
> **Pet Fee**: $30 per night per room
>
> **Refundable Pet Deposit**: $150
>
> **Size Limit**: None
>
> **Terms**: Adult dogs only. Dogs must be leashed at all times. Pets may not be left unattended in rooms. Owners must pick up after their pets, pick up bags are available. Advance reservations required.
>
> **Pet Amenities**: Doggie dishes and a dog blanket are provided. Plenty of grassy areas to walk your pet.
>
> **Fido's Favorite Features**: Great location to ski and stay, comfortable accommodations, pet-friendly staff.

Village Hotel at The Village
at Breckenridge Resort
535 South Park Avenue 80424
970-547-5725 / 800-832-4025

> **Restaurant**: Park Avenue Pub
>
> **H20**: Year round indoor/outdoor pool, indoor & outdoor hot tubs.
>
> **Pet Fee**: $30 per night per room
>
> **Refundable Pet Deposit**: $150
>
> **Size Limit**: None
>
> **Terms**: Adult dogs only. Dogs must be leashed at all times. Pets may not be left unattended in rooms. Owners must pick up after their pets, pick up bags are available. Advanced reservations required.
>
> **Pet Amenities**: Doggie dishes and a dog blanket are provided. Plenty of grassy areas to walk your pet.

Wildwood Suites
120 Sawmill Road 80424
970-453-0232 / 800-866-0300

> **Restaurant**: Walking distance to several restaurants.
>
> **H20**: Two outdoor hot tubs
>
> **Pet Fee**: $75 one time fee per stay
>
> **Refundable Pet Deposit**: None
>
> **Size Limit**: None
>
> **Terms**: One well-behaved dog per room. One bedroom condos only.
>
> **Pet Amenities**: Plenty of space to walk pets on property. Pet pick up bags available at front desk.

-Broomfield-

Omni Interlocken Resort
500 Interlocken Boulevard 80021
303-438-6600 / 800-THE-OMNI

> **Restaurant**: The Meritage, The Tap Room, Fairways Restaurant
>
> **H20**: Outdoor pool and hot tub
>
> **Pet Fee**: None
>
> **Refundable Pet Deposit**: $50

Size Limit: 50 lbs.

Terms: Well-behaved pets welcome.

Pet Amenities: Dog treats upon check in. There are pet walking areas on the property. See the Concierge for details about local services available.

Fido's Favorite Features: The pool area, The Omni Spa, the fantastic golf courses, the luxurious accommodations. Located near the pet-friendly & fabulous Flatiron Crossing Mall. There are plenty of options to keep you busy at this gorgeous destination resort.

TownePlace Suites
by Marriott Boulder/Broomfield
480 Flatiron Boulevard 80021
303-466-2200 / 800-257-3000

> **Restaurant**: Walking distance
>
> **H20**: Seasonal outdoor pool
>
> **Pet Fee**: $75 one time fee per stay
>
> **Refundable Pet Deposit**: None
>
> **Size Limit**: 75 lbs.
>
> **Terms**: Pets must be house trained and well-behaved.
>
> **Pet Amenities**: Pet treats at front desk. Flexible housekeeping to accommodate guest's schedule with pets. Pet walk area on property.

-Brush-

Best Value Inn Brush
1208 North Colorado Avenue 80723
970-842-5146

> **Restaurant**: Walking distance
>
> **H20**: Seasonal outdoor pool
>
> **Pet Fee**: $10 per day per pet
>
> **Refundable Pet Deposit**: None
>
> **Size Limit**: None
>
> **Terms**: Pets cannot be left in room unattended. Cats must be in a carrier. No birds.
>
> **Pet Amenities**: Pet walking area on west side of building.

-Buena Vista-

Best Western Vista Inn
733 U.S. Highway 24 North 81211
719-395-8009 / 800-809-3495

> **Restaurant**: Walking distance to several restaurants.
>
> **H20**: Indoor pool and hot tub, two seasonal outdoor hot tubs
>
> **Pet Fee**: $7 per pet per night
>
> **Refundable Pet Deposit**: $50

Size Limit: None

Terms: Pets cannot be left in room unattended. No cats. No more than two dogs per room.

Pet Amenities: A pet treat at check in. Ample walking area on property.

-Burlington-

Burlington Comfort Inn
282 S. Lincoln Street 80807
719-346-7676 / 888-388-7676

> **Restaurant**: Walking distance
> **H20**: Indoor pool and hot tub
> **Pet Fee**: $10 per day per pet
> **Refundable Pet Deposit**: $50
> **Size Limit**: None
> **Terms**: Well-behaved pets welcome.
> **Pet Amenities**: Grassy areas both in front and behind building.

Chaparral Motor Inn
405 South Lincoln Street 80807
719-346-5361

> **Restaurant**: Several within walking distance.
> **H20**: Seasonal outdoor pool
> **Pet Fee**: $7 per day per room
> **Refundable Pet Deposit**: None
> **Size Limit**: None
> **Terms**: Pets cannot be left in room unattended.
> **Pet Amenities**: Grassy areas on both sides of buildings for walking pets.

No matter how much they look like they want it, chocolate is toxic to dogs. So don't give it to them.

-Canon City-

Best Western Royal Gorge Motel
1925 Fremont Drive 81212
719-275-3377 / 800-231-7317

Restaurant: Crystal's Family Diner

H20: Seasonal outdoor pool, year round gazebo hot tub

Pet Fee: $15 per stay per room

Refundable Pet Deposit: None

Size Limit: None

Terms: Well-behaved pets welcome. Pets need to be crated if left in room unattended.

Pet Amenities: Pet walking area on property. Pet-friendly staff.

Comfort Inn
311 Royal Gorge Boulevard 81212
719-276-6900 / 800-4CHOICE

Restaurant: Walking distance

H20: Indoor pool and hot tub

Pet Fee: $10 per stay per room

Refundable Pet Deposit: None

Size Limit: None

Terms: Limited to domestic pets. No pot-bellied pigs or miniature horses.

Pet Amenities: There is a park conveniently located across the street. Pet waste bags are available at the front desk. The house dog is usually at the front desk to greet you. Pets are allowed in any room.

Holiday Inn Express
110 Latigo Lane 81212
719-275-2400 / 877-422-6665

Restaurant: Walking distance

H20: Indoor pool and hot tub

Pet Fee: $15 per stay per pet

Refundable Pet Deposit: None

Size Limit: Prefer small pets

Terms: Only 3 pet rooms. Call in advance for availability.

Pet Amenities: Grassy area to walk your pets.

Quality Inn & Suites
3075 East Hwy 50 81212
719-275-8676 / 800-525-7727

Restaurant: Duke's Restaurant, True Grit Lounge

H20: Year round outdoor pool, five indoor hot tubs.

Pet Fee: None

Refundable Pet Deposit: None

Size Limit: None

Terms: Pet rooms are on the first floor with convenient outdoor access.

Pet Amenities: Pet walking area on property.

-Carbondale-

Comfort Inn & Suites
920 Cowen Drive 81623
970-963-8880 / 800-473-5980

Restaurant: Walking distance

H20: Indoor pool and hot tub

Pet Fee: $10 per pet per night

Refundable Pet Deposit: None

Size Limit: 75 lbs.

Terms: Pets cannot be left in room unattended unless crated.

Pet Amenities: Designated pet walking area behind hotel.
 Pet pick up bags and pet welcome letter at check in.

Take the time to stop and exercise your pooch while traveling long distances. He will be less restless and more likely to relax.

Days Inn-Carbondale
950 Cowen Drive 81623
970-963-9111 / 800-944-3297

> **Restaurant**: Walking distance
>
> **H20**: Indoor pool and hot tub
>
> **Pet Fee**: $8 per pet per day
>
> **Refundable Pet Deposit**: None
>
> **Size Limit**: None
>
> **Terms**: Pets cannot be left in the room unattended.
>
> **Pet Amenities**: Open field next to the building to walk your dogs.

-Castle Rock-

Best Western Inn & Suites of Castle Rock
595 Genoa Way 80109
303-814-8800 / 800-WESTERN

> **Restaurant**: IHOP
>
> **H20**: Indoor pool and hot tub
>
> **Pet Fee**: $15 per pet per day
>
> **Refundable Pet Deposit**: None
>
> **Size Limit**: 50 lbs.
>
> **Terms**: Pets cannot be left in room unattended. Pets are not allowed in lobby area. Pet rooms are on the second floor.
>
> **Pet Amenities**: Grassy areas to walk your pets on property.
>
> * Don't forget to visit the fabulous upscale / high quality pet supply store, *The Pet Stuff Place*. Your pets will thank you.

Comfort Suites
4755 Castleton Way 80104
303-814-9999 / 800-4CHOICE

Restaurant: Walking distance

H20: Indoor pool and hot tub

Pet Fee: $10 per room per day

Refundable Pet Deposit: None

Size Limit: None

Terms: Pets must be well-behaved.

Pet Amenities: Plenty of room to walk pets on property.

Holiday Inn Express
884 Park Street 80104
303-660-9733   800-HOLIDAY

Restaurant: Walking distance

H20: Indoor pool and hot tub

Pet Fee: $10 per night per pet

Size Limit: None

Terms: Pets cannot be left in room unattended.

Pet Amenities: Plenty of areas to walk pets on property.

-Cedaredge-

Howard Johnson Express Inn
530 S. Grand Mesa Drive 81413
970-856-7824 / 888-855-2700

Restaurant: Short drive

H20: Indoor pool and hot tub

Pet Fee: $10 per day per pet

Refundable Pet Deposit: $10 cash deposit or credit card

Size Limit: None

Terms: Pets cannot be left unattended in room.

Pet Amenities: There is a walking path along a creek near the property.

-Centennial-

Embassy Suites Denver Tech Center
10250 East Costilla Avenue 80112
303-792-0433 / 800-EMBASSY

Restaurant: New West Grill

H20: Indoor pool and hot tub

Pet Fee: $75

Refundable Pet Deposit: None

Size Limit: 140 lbs.

Terms: Well-behaved pets welcome. Barkers cannot be left alone in room. Housekeeping will not enter room unless pet is crated.

Pet Amenities: Walking trail located behind the property.

Fido's Favorite Features: Fantastic accommodations, spacious suites, convenient location.

-Colorado City-

Days Inn
6670 Highway 165 81019
719-676-2340 / 800-DAYS-INN

Restaurant: Days Inn Restaurant

H20: Indoor pool

Pet Fee: None

Refundable Pet Deposit: None

Size Limit: None

Terms: Make prior arrangements for housekeeping if dog is left in room.

Pet Amenities: Dog treats at check in. There is a large field in back to walk pets.

Many public parks have receptacles which provide complimentary "doggie do bags".

-Colorado Springs-

Amerisuites Colorado Springs
Garden of the Gods

503 W. Garden of the Gods Road 80907
719-265-9385 / 800-833-1516

Restaurant: Within walking distance

H20: Seasonal outdoor pool

Pet Fee: $10 per pet per night

Refundable Pet Deposit: None

Size Limit: None

Terms: Guest is responsible for any damages caused by pets.

Pet Amenities: Grassy areas on property for walking pet.

Best Western Airport Inn
1780 Aeroplaza Drive 80916
719-574-7707 / 866-740-3824

> **Restaurant**: Walking distance
>
> **H20**: Indoor pool and hot tub
>
> **Pet Fee**: $10 per night per pet
>
> **Refundable Pet Deposit**: $25
>
> **Size Limit**: None
>
> **Terms**: Pets cannot be left unattended in room. Guest is responsible for damages. Pet rooms are all smoking rooms.
>
> **Pet Amenities**: Ample walking area on property.

Best Western Executive Inn & Suites
1440 Harrison Road 80906
719-576-2371 / 800-WESTERN

> **Restaurant**: Several within walking distance
>
> **H20**: Indoor pool and hot tub
>
> **Pet Fee**: $10 per night per pet
>
> **Refundable Pet Deposit**: None
>
> **Size Limit**: None
>
> **Terms**: Two dogs maximum per room
>
> **Pet Amenities**: Grassy areas on property to walk pets.

Best Western Pikes Peak Inn
3010 North Chestnut Street 80907
719-636-5201 / 800-WESTERN

> **Restaurant**: Best Western Pikes Peak Restaurant (summer only)
>
> **H20**: Seasonal outdoor pool
>
> **Pet Fee**: $10 per pet per day
>
> **Refundable Pet Deposit**: None
>
> **Size Limit**: Prefer small pets.
>
> **Terms**: Pets cannot be left unattended in room.
>
> **Pet Amenities**: Pet walking area behind property.

"Dogs are not our whole lives, but they make our lives whole."
-Roger Caras

Comfort Inn South World Arena
1410 Harrison Road 80906
719-579-6900 / 800-4CHOICE

> **Restaurant**: Several within walking distance
>
> **H20**: Indoor pool and hot tub
>
> **Pet Fee**: None
>
> **Refundable Pet Deposit**: $25
>
> **Size Limit**: None
>
> **Terms**: Pets cannot be left in room unattended unless crated. Pets must be in smoking rooms.
>
> **Pet Amenities**: Grassy areas on property to walk pets.

Comfort Suites & Sleep Inn
1055 Kelly Johnson Blvd. 80920
719-536-0731 \ 888-515-3131

> **Restaurant**: Within walking distance.
>
> **H20**: Indoor pool, year round outdoor pool and hot tub.
>
> **Pet Fee**: $10 per night per room
>
> **Refundable Pet Deposit**: None
>
> **Size Limit**: None
>
> **Terms**: Pets must be in smoking rooms.
>
> **Pet Amenities**: Large field behind properties to walk pets.

Days Inn - Air Force Academy
8350 Razorback Road 80920
719-266-1317 / 800-329-7466

> **Restaurant**: Several within walking distance
>
> **H20**: Indoor pool and hot tub
>
> **Pet Fee**: $10 per night per pet
>
> **Refundable Pet Deposit**: None
>
> **Size Limit**: None
>
> **Terms**: Pets cannot be left in room unattended.
>
> **Pet Amenities**: Plenty of space to walk pets around property.

"Dojjeez" - Claire Bellamy

Everything I need to recharge my life.
My Homewood.

It's easier to enjoy quality time together when you have more room to spread out. At Homewood Suites by Hilton®, you'll find two-room suites* with fully equipped kitchens and complimentary hot breakfast. And the family pet can come along, too. Just visit homewoodsuites.com or call 1-800-CALL-HOME®.

MAKE YOURSELF AT HOME.™

Homewood Suites by Hilton
9130 Explorer Dr
Colorado Springs CO 80920
719-265-6600

Homewood Suites by Hilton
4950 Baseline Rd
Boulder CO 80303
303-499-9922

Doubletree Hotel World Arena

1775 E. Cheyenne Mountain Boulevard 80906
719-576-8900 / 800-222-8733

>**Restaurant**: Atrium Cafe
>
>**H20**: Indoor pool and hot tub
>
>**Pet Fee**: $10 per day per pet
>
>**Refundable Pet Deposit**: None
>
>**Size Limit**: None
>
>**Terms**: Pets cannot be left unattended in room.
>
>**Pet Amenities**: Nice walking area on property.
>
>**Fido's Favorite Features**: Comfortable rooms, nice pool area, accommodating staff. This very nice Doubletree Hotel is conveniently located right off I-25.

Drury Inn Pikes Peak

8155 N. Academy Boulevard 80920
719-598-2500 / 800-DRURYINN

>**Restaurant**: Walking distance to several
>
>**H20**: Indoor/outdoor pool and hot tub
>
>**Pet Fee**: None
>
>**Refundable Pet Deposit**: None
>
>**Size Limit**: None
>
>**Terms**: Pet cannot be left unattended in the room. No more than one pet per room. Must sign pet agreement.
>
>**Pet Amenities**: Grassy areas on property to walk pets.

Econo Lodge Inn & Suites World Arena

1623 South Nevada Avenue 80906
719-632-6651 / 800-553-2666

>**Restaurant**: Several within walking distance
>
>**H20**: Seasonal outdoor pool
>
>**Pet Fee**: $10 per stay per room
>
>**Refundable Pet Deposit**: $10
>
>**Size Limit**: None
>
>**Terms**: Pets cannot be left unattended in room.
>
>**Pet Amenities**: Designated dog walking area. Pet pick up bags available.

Homewood Suites by Hilton

9130 Explorer Drive 80920

719-265-6600 / 800-225-5466

> **Restaurant**: Walking distance to several restaurants.
>
> **H20**: Seasonal outdoor pool
>
> **Pet Fee**: $25 per stay per pet.
>
> **Refundable Pet Deposit**: None
>
> **Size Limit**: None
>
> **Terms**: Must remove pet or make arrangements with housekeeping.
>
> **Pet Amenities**: Bowl with dog treats at check in. Pet sitting services can be arranged through the front desk.
>
> **Fido's Favorite Features**: Pet-friendly staff, lots of grass for walking pets, Immaculate rooms.

Homewood Suites by Hilton Colorado Springs Airport

2875 Zeppelin Road 80916

719-574-2701 / 800-225-5466

> **Restaurant**: Short drive
>
> **H20**: Indoor pool and hot tub
>
> **Pet Fee**: $50 per room per stay
>
> **Refundable Pet Deposit**: None
>
> **Size Limit**: 50 lbs.
>
> **Terms**: Pets must be crated if left in room unattended.
>
> **Pet Amenities**: Designated pet walking area.

La Quinta Inn & Suites Colorado Springs Airport

2750 Geyser Drive 80906

719-527-4788 / 800-531-5900

> **Restaurant**: Several within walking distance.
>
> **H20**: Outdoor hot tub, seasonal outdoor pool.
>
> **Pet Fee**: None
>
> **Refundable Pet Deposit**: None
>
> **Size Limit**: 35 lbs.
>
> **Terms**: Owners must pick up after pets. Pets cannot be left in room unattended.
>
> **Pet Amenities**: Grassy areas on property to walk your pets.

La Quinta Inn, Garden of the Gods
4385 Sinton Rd. 80907
719-528-5060 / 800-531-5900
> **Restaurant**: Walking distance
> **H20**: Seasonal outdoor pool
> **Pet Fee**: None
> **Refundable Pet Deposit**: None
> **Size Limit**: 30 lbs.
> **Terms**: Pets cannot be left in room unattended.
> **Pet Amenities**: There is a nice walking trail nearby.

Le Baron Hotel Downtown Colorado Springs
314 West Bijou Street 80905
719-471-8680 / 800-477-8610
> **Restaurant**: Riley's Restaurant
> **H20**: Seasonal outdoor pool and hot tub
> **Pet Fee**: None
> **Refundable Pet Deposit**: $50
> **Size Limit**: None
> **Terms**: Pets cannot be left in room unattended unless crated.
> **Pet Amenities**: Area to walk your pet on property.

Park Plaza
505 Popes Bluff Trail 80907
719-598-7656 / 800-814-7000
> **Restaurant**: Morgan's
> **H20**: Outdoor hot tub and seasonal outdoor pool
> **Pet Fee**: None
> **Refundable Pet Deposit**: $50
> **Size Limit**: 50 lbs.
> **Terms**: Pets cannot be left unattended in room. One pet per room maximum. Pets must be house-trained.
> **Pet Amenities**: Grassy areas on property to walk pets.

Quality Inn - Garden of the Gods
555 West Garden of the Gods Road 80907
719-593-9119 / 800-828-4347

> **Restaurant**: Several within walking distance
>
> **H20**: Seasonal outdoor pool
>
> **Pet Fee**: None
>
> **Refundable Pet Deposit**: $50
>
> **Size Limit**: None
>
> **Terms**: Pets must be leashed while in common areas.
>
> **Pet Amenities**: There are grassy areas on property to walk pets.

Radisson Inn & Suites
Colorado Springs Airport
1645 North Newport Road 80916
719-597-7000 / 800-333-3333

> **Restaurant**: Bistro Colorado
>
> **H20**: Indoor pool and outdoor hot tub
>
> **Pet Fee**: $25 per pet per stay
>
> **Refundable Pet Deposit**: $100
>
> **Size Limit**: 50 lbs.
>
> **Terms**: Guests must sign a pet policy agreement upon check in. Pets must be crated if left in room unattended. Two pet maximum per room.
>
> **Pet Amenities**: Nice pet walk area behind hotel.
>
> **Fido's Favorite Features**: Convenient location, friendly staff, Bistro Colorado. This is a fantastic place to stay if you need accommodations near the Colorado Springs airport.

Ramada Limited East - Airport
520 North Murray Blvd. 80915
719-596-7660 / 800-2RAMADA

> **Restaurant**: Short drive
>
> **H20**: Indoor pool and hot tub
>
> **Pet Fee**: $5 per pet per day
>
> **Refundable Pet Deposit**: $20
>
> **Size Limit**: None
>
> **Terms**: Pets cannot be left unattended in room.
>
> **Pet Amenities**: Pet walking area on property.

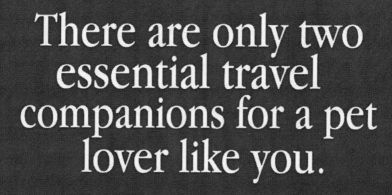

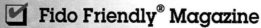
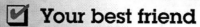

Residence Inn Central Colorado Springs
3880 N. Academy Boulevard 80917
719-574-0370 / 800-331-3131

> **Restaurant**: Walking distance
> **H20**: Seasonal outdoor pool
> **Pet Fee**: $75 one time fee
> **Refundable Pet Deposit**: None
> **Size Limit**: None
> **Terms**: The pet fee is used to deep clean the room upon check out.
> **Pet Amenities**: Dog treats at check in. Pet walking / care can be arranged through the front desk.

Residence Inn North Colorado Springs
9805 Federal Drive 80921
719-388-9300 / 800-331-3131

> **Restaurant**: Short drive
> **H20**: Indoor pool and hot tub
> **Pet Fee**: $75 for the first day and after, $5 additional per day
> **Refundable Pet Deposit**: $50 cash or credit card
> **Size Limit**: None
> **Terms**: Must make arrangements with housekeeping for service.
> **Pet Amenities**. There are grassy areas nearby to walk pets.

Residence Inn South Colorado Springs
2765 Geyser Drive 80906
719-576-0101 / 800-331-3131

> **Restaurant**: Walking distance
> **H20**: Indoor pool and hot tub
> **Pet Fee**: $75 one time fee per stay
> **Refundable Pet Deposit**: $50 cash or credit card
> **Size Limit**: None
> **Terms**: Must make arrangements with housekeeping for service.
> **Pet Amenities**: Dog or cat treats at check in.

"None are as fiercely loyal as dog people."
-Linda Shrieves

Sheraton Hotel Colorado Springs
2886 South Circle Drive 80906
719-576-5900 / 800-981-4012

>**Restaurant**: Café Terracotta, The Country Store, Rickenbacker's Bar & Grille
>
>**H20**: Indoor pool and hot tub, seasonal outdoor pool
>
>**Pet Fee**: None
>
>**Refundable Pet Deposit**: $50
>
>**Size Limit**: 75 lbs.
>
>**Terms**: Well-behaved pets welcome.
>
>**Pet Amenities**: Pet beds available. Areas to walk pets on property.
>
>**Fido's Favorite Features**: Convenient location, comfortable accommodations, pet-friendly staff.

Staybridge Suites - Air Force Academy
7130 Commerce Center Drive 80919
719-590-7829 / 800-215-0090

>**Restaurant**: Several within walking distance.
>
>**H20**: Outdoor seasonal pool and hot tub
>
>**Pet Fee**: $150 per stay per pet
>
>**Refundable Pet Deposit**: None
>
>**Size Limit**: None
>
>**Terms**: Pet rooms are on the first floor.
>
>**Pet Amenities**: There is plenty of space to walk pets on property.

TownePlace Suites by Marriott
4760 Centennial Boulevard 80919
719-594-4447 / 800-257-3000

>**Restaurant**: Walking distance
>
>**H20**: Seasonal outdoor pool
>
>**Pet Fee**: $20 per day/ $200 maximum per stay
>
>**Refundable Pet Deposit**: None
>
>**Size Limit**: None
>
>**Terms**: Pets must be house trained and well-behaved.
>
>**Pet Amenities**: Pet walking area on property. Pet treats at check in. Flexible housekeeping to accommodate guest's schedule with pets.

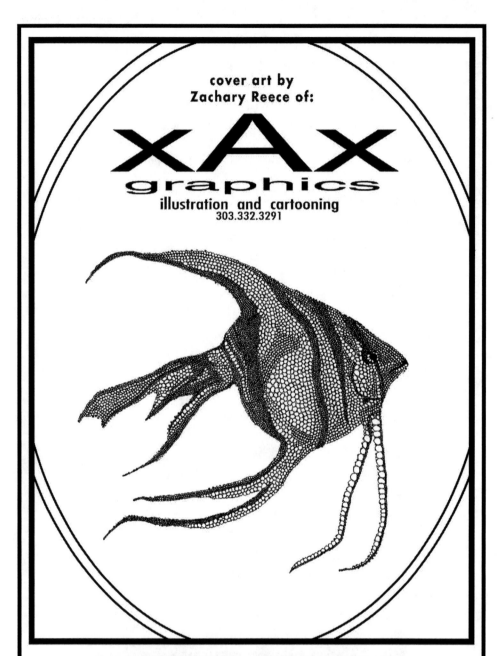

Travelodge
2625 Ore Mill Road 80904
719-632-4600 / 800-578-7878

Restaurant: Short drive

H20: Indoor pool

Pet Fee: $20 per room per stay

Refundable Pet Deposit: None

Size Limit: None

Terms: Pets cannot be left in room unattended.

Pet Amenities: Pet walking area on property.

Wyndham Hotel Colorado Springs
5580 Tech Center Drive 80919
719-260-1800 / 800-WYNDHAM

Restaurant: Gratzi

H20: Indoor pool and hot tub, seasonal outdoor pool

Pet Fee: $25 one time fee per pet per stay

Refundable Pet Deposit: $250

Size Limit: None

Terms: Pets cannot be left in room unattended.

Pet Amenities: There is a nice walking trail behind the hotel.

Fido's Favorite Features: Nice outdoor pool area, great bath products, Gratzi.

* Don't miss The Natural Pet Market and Self Serve Dog Wash. Your dog might not forgive you if you don't bring him by for a scrub, a sniff, a snack and a toy.

Road Trippin'

-Copper Mountain-

Copper Mountain Resort
509 Copper Road 80443
970-968-2882 / 866-837-2997

Restaurant: Several within walking distance.

H20: Includes use of the athletic club at Copper Mountain, which has an indoor swimming pool and hot tubs.

Pet Fee: $15 per night per pet

Refundable Pet Deposit: $40

Size Limit: None

Terms: Pets cannot be left in room unattended unless crated. Pets must be leashed in common areas. Owner is responsible to pick up after pets.

Pet Amenities: Plenty of room to walk pets in area.

-Cortez-

Anasazi Motor Inn
640 South Broadway 81321
970-565-3773 / 800-972-6232

Restaurant: Anasazi Restaurant

H20: Seasonal outdoor pool and outdoor year round hot tub

Pet Fee: None

Refundable Pet Deposit: $50

Size Limit: 40 lbs.

Terms: Pets cannot be left in room unattended.

Pet Amenities: Pet walking area and walking path behind property.

Bring a recent photo of your pet in case he gets lost.

Best Western Turquoise Inn & Suites
535 E. Main Street 81321
970-565-3778 / 800-547-3376

Restaurant: Walking distance

H20: Indoor hot tub, seasonal outdoor pool

Pet Fee: $15 per room per stay

Refundable Pet Deposit: None

Size Limit: None

Terms: Guest must pick up after pets.

Pet Amenities: City Park is two blocks away for exercising pets.

Budget Host Inn
2040 East Main Street 81321
970-565-3738 / 888-677-3738

Restaurant: Walking distance

H20: Seasonal outdoor pool and indoor year round hot tub

Pet Fee: $5 per pet per day

Refundable Pet Deposit: None

Size Limit: None

Terms: Well-behaved pets welcome

Pet Amenities: Grassy areas to walk your pets on property.

Comfort Inn
2321 E. Main Street 81321
970-565-3400 / 800-4CHOICE

Restaurant: Walking distance

H20: Indoor pool and hot tub

Pet Fee: $10 per room per stay

Refundable Pet Deposit: None

Size Limit: None

Terms: Guest is responsible for any damages caused by pets. Guest must make arrangements with housekeeping to have room serviced.

Pet Amenities: Pet walking area on property.

Days Inn
US Hwy 160 at State 145 81321
970-565-8577 / 800-DAYS-INN
> **Restaurant**: Walking distance
> **H20**: Seasonal outdoor pool
> **Pet Fee**: $10 per room per stay
> **Refundable Pet Deposit**: None
> **Size Limit**: None
> **Terms**: Housekeeping will not enter room if pet is left unattended.
> **Pet Amenities**: Plenty of space to walk pets.

Holiday Inn Express
2121 East Main Street 81321
970-565-6000 / 800-626-5652
> **Restaurant**: Walking distance
> **H20**: Indoor pool and hot tub
> **Pet Fee**: None
> **Refundable Pet Deposit**: None
> **Size Limit**: 50 lbs.
> **Terms**: Must sign pet policy agreement form at check in. Must request a pet room when making reservations. Pets cannot be left in room unattended.
> **Pet Amenities**: Pet walking area in back of building. Dog biscuits at check in.

Travelodge
440 South Broadway 81321
970-565-7778 / 800-578-7878
> **Restaurant**: Walking distance
> **H20**: Seasonal outdoor pool, indoor hot tub
> **Pet Fee**: $5 per day per pet
> **Refundable Pet Deposit**: None
> **Size Limit**: Prefer small pets
> **Terms**: Pets cannot be left in room unattended.
> **Pet Amenities**: Pet walk area on property.

-Craig-

Holiday Inn
300 South Colorado Highway 13 81625
970-824-4000 / 800-HOLIDAY

    Restaurant: Paradise Grill and Cassidy's Lounge

    H20: Indoor pool and hot tub

    Pet Fee: None

    Refundable Pet Deposit: $50 cash or credit card

    Size Limit: None

    Terms: Well-behaved pets are welcome.

    Pet Amenities: Dog treats at check in. There is a large grassy area for walking pets.

-Creede-

Snowshoe Lodge
202 East 8th Street 81130
719-658-2315 / 866-658-2315

    Restaurant: Walking distance

    H20: None

    Pet Fee: $10 per pet per day

    Refundable Pet Deposit: None

    Size Limit: None

    Terms: Well-behaved pets are welcome.

    Pet Amenities: Ample walking areas in pet friendly downtown Creede.

When traveling long distances, bring a fairly large Tupperware dish with a tight fitting lid. First thing each morning, fill the Tupperware with mostly ice and a little water. While traveling, if your pooch needs a drink, his convenient dish of cold water is waiting for him.

-Crested Butte-

The Elizabeth Anne B&B 🐾 🐾 🐾
703 Maroon Avenue 81224
970-349-0147 / 888-745-4620

Restaurant: Several within walking distance

H20: Indoor hot tub

Pet Fee: None

Refundable Pet Deposit: None

Size Limit: None

Terms: No puppies please.

Pet Amenities: Pet treats, doggie blankets.

Fido's Favorite Features: Great location, pet-friendly B&B, close to hiking trails.

The Grand Lodge Crested Butte 🐾 🐾 🐾 🐾
6 Emmons Loop Mt. Crested Butte 81225
970-349-8000 / 800-823-4446

Restaurant: The Woodstone Grille

H20: Year round indoor/outdoor pool, outdoor hot tub

Pet Fee: $30 per day per room

Refundable Pet Deposit: None

Size Limit: None

Terms: Four dogs per room maximum.

Pet Amenities: Concierge or front desk can direct you to endless pet-friendly hiking and cross country skiing trails.

Fido's Favorite Features: Great location for hikers and skiers, nice pool area, free town shuttle is just steps from the hotel.

Old Town Inn

708 6th Street 81224
970-349-6184 / 888-349-6184

Restaurant: Several within walking distance

H20: Outdoor hot tub

Pet Fee: $10 per night per room

Refundable Pet Deposit: None

Size Limit: None

Terms: Pets cannot be left in room unattended.

Pet Amenities: Great walking trails right out your door.

"I think dogs are the most amazing creatures; they give unconditional love. For me, they are the role model for being alive." -Gilda Radner

The Pioneer Guest Cabins

2094 County Road 740 81224

970-349-5517

Restaurant: Short drive

H20: None

Pet Fee: $10 per pet per night

Refundable Pet Deposit: $100

Size Limit: None

Terms: No Pit Bulls, Rottwielers or German Shepherds. Pets cannot be left unattended in cabins. 2 dog maximum. Pets must be on a leash while in public areas.

Pet Amenities: Miles of trails right from cabin door. Cement Creek for your dogs to swim.

"Every dog must have his day."

-Jonathon Swift

The Purple Mountain Lodge B&B
714 Gothic Avenue 81224
970-349-5888 / 800-759-9066

Restaurant: Several within walking distance

H20: Outdoor hot tub

Pet Fee: $10 per night per pet

Refundable Pet Deposit: None

Size Limit: None

Terms: Well-behaved pets welcome.

Pet Amenities: Close to miles of hiking trails. Steps from the Gunnison National Forest, ample lakes and streams galore!

Fido's Favorite Features: An Essential Escape Spa offers incredible skin and massage treatments, including what could be described as The World's Best Facial. Great downtown location, comfortable accommodations, pet-friendly!

*Mountain Tails is a fantastic, quality pet supply store right in the center of town on Elk Avenue. Bring your leashed pet by for fresh baked treats, the latest in pet fashion, outdoor gear and everything Fido has in mind.

THE GRAND LODGE
CRESTED BUTTE
HOTEL & SUITES

888-823-4446 • www.grandlodgecrestedbutte.com • 6 Emmons Loop • Mt. Crested Butte, CO 81225

Stay at the only full service hotel in Crested Butte!

Let us take the stress out of your next vacation!

❋ Luxurious yet affordable.
❋ Located less than 200 yards from ski lifts
❋ 5 million dollar renovation completed summer 2004.
❋ Open all summer from Memorial Day through Halloween, all winter through ski season.

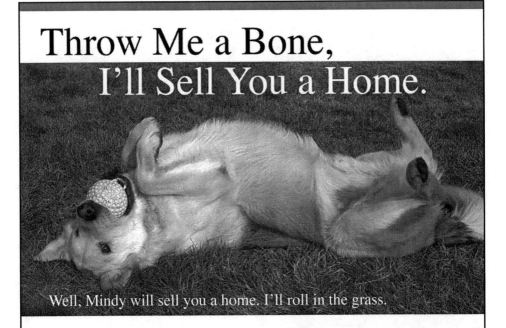

The Ruby of Crested Butte B&B
624 Gothic Avenue 81224
970-349-1338 / 800-390-1338

> **Restaurant**: Several within walking distance
>
> **H20**: Indoor hot tub
>
> **Pet Fee**: None
>
> **Refundable Pet Deposit**: None
>
> **Size Limit**: None
>
> **Terms**: Please go to www.therubyofcrestedbutte.com for more information.
>
> **Pet Amenities**: The house dog River welcomes you! Pet sitting/walking service available. Homemade healthy dog treats, dog dishes for food and water, comfy dog beds and blankets. Doggie Concierge can arrange pet spa treatments, grooming and more.
>
> **Fido's Favorite Features**: Very pet-friendly! Delicious gourmet breakfast, deluxe accommodations, convenient location.

-Cripple Creek-

Double Eagle Hotel & Casino
442 East Bennett Avenue 80813
719-689-5000 / 800-711-7234

> **Restaurant**: Lombards, The Deli, The Winfield
>
> **H20**: None
>
> **Pet Fee**: $50
>
> **Refundable Pet Deposit**: $50
>
> **Size Limit**: None
>
> **Terms**: Well-behaved pets welcome. Owner is responsible for pet's behavior.
>
> **Pet Amenities**: Pet walking area across the street from hotel.

Watch out for cactus in many parts of Colorado.

-Cuchara-

Dodgeton Creek Inn
90 East Cuchara Avenue 81055
719-742-5169
> **Restaurant**: Short drive
>
> **H20**: None
>
> **Pet Fee**: None
>
> **Refundable Pet Deposit**: None
>
> **Size Limit**: None
>
> **Terms**: Well-behaved pets are welcome.
>
> **Pet Amenities**: Property is located on the banks of Dodgeton Creek for your pet's swimming pleasure.

River's Edge B&B
90 East Cuchara Avenue 81055
719-742-5169
> **Restaurant**: Short drive
>
> **H20**: None
>
> **Pet Fee**: None
>
> **Refundable Pet Deposit**: None
>
> **Size Limit**: None
>
> **Terms**: Well-behaved pets are welcome.
>
> **Pet Amenities**: Property is located on the banks of Dodgeton Creek for your pet's swimming pleasure.

-Delta-

Best Western Sundance Inn
903 Main Street 81416
970-874-9781 / 800-626-1994
> **Restaurant**: Sundance Restaurant
>
> **H20**: Indoor hot tub, seasonal outdoor pool
>
> **Pet Fee**: $5 per day per pet
>
> **Refundable Pet Deposit**: None

Size Limit: None

Terms: None

Pet Amenities: Grassy areas around the property and neighborhood.

Delta Comfort Inn
180 Gunnison River Drive 81416
970-874-1000 / 800-249-5717

Restaurant: Walking distance

H20: Access to public recreation center, $2 for adults, $1 for children.

Pet Fee: $10 per day per pet

Refundable Pet Deposit: None

Size Limit: None

Terms: Pets must be leashed in public areas.

Pet Amenities: Confluence Park has walking trails and is located on the banks of the Gunnison River. The park is located behind this Comfort Inn.

South Gate Inn
2124 South Main Street 81416
970-874-9726 / 800-621-2271

Restaurant: Short drive

H20: Seasonal outdoor pool and year round outdoor hot tub

Pet Fee: $5 per day per room

Refundable Pet Deposit: None

Size Limit: None

Terms: Well-mannered pets welcome.

Pet Amenities: There is plenty of room to walk pets around property.

High altitude not only effects humans, but our pets as well. Keep your pets hydrated with plenty of water.

-Denver-

The Brown Palace Hotel
321 17th Street 80202
303-297-3111 / 800-321-2599

Restaurant: Ellyngton's, Palace Arms, Ship Tavern

H20: None

Pet Fee: $50 per stay per pet

Refundable Pet Deposit: None

Size Limit: None

Terms: Well-behaved pets welcome.

Pet Amenities: Dog bed, dog bowl, a "bone appetit" welcome treat at check in. Dog walking services available.

Fido's Favorite Features: Beautiful lobby, impressive accommodations, excellent restaurants. This luxurious hotel's staff is at your service to make sure you have a top-notch experience.

"Nothing but the best for my puppy."
-Frank Zappa

Cherry Creek Hotel
1475 South Colorado Blvd. 80222
303-757-8797

> **Restaurant**: Within walking distance.
>
> **H20**: Indoor pool
>
> **Pet Fee**: None
>
> **Refundable Pet Deposit**: None
>
> **Size Limit**: None
>
> **Terms**: Well-behaved pets welcome.
>
> **Pet Amenities**: Grassy areas nearby to walk your pet.

Comfort Inn Downtown Denver
401 17th Street 80202
303-296-0400 / 800-4CHOICE

> **Restaurant**: Several within walking distance.
>
> **H20**: None
>
> **Pet Fee**: $100 per stay per room
>
> **Refundable Pet Deposit**: None
>
> **Size Limit**: 25 lbs.
>
> **Terms**: Pets cannot be left in room unattended.
>
> **Pet Amenities**: Small park near the hotel for walking pets.

Denver Marriott Tech Center
4900 S. Syracuse 80237
303-779-1100 / 800-228-9290

> **Restaurant**: Comparis, The Great Divide
>
> **H20**: Indoor pool and hot tub, seasonal outdoor pool
>
> **Pet Fee**: $50
>
> **Refundable Pet Deposit**: None
>
> **Size Limit**: 50 lbs.
>
> **Terms**: Pets cannot be left unattended in room. No puppies allowed.
>
> **Pet Amenities**: Grassy areas on property.
>
> **Fido's Favorite Features**: Comfortable beds, nice accomodations. Plenty of room to walk your pets. Convenient location near the Tech Center.

Doubletree Hotel Denver

3203 Quebec Street 80207

303-321-3333   800-222-TREE

> **Restaurant**: The Cafe, Characters Sports Bar & Grill
>
> **H20**: Indoor pool, outdoor hot tub
>
> **Pet Fee**: $20 per stay per room
>
> **Refundable Pet Deposit**: None
>
> **Size Limit**: None
>
> **Terms**: Well-behaved pets only
>
> **Pet Amenities**: Grassy areas on property for walking pets.
>
> **Fido's Favorite Features**: Friendly staff, comfortable accommodations, Convenient location off I70. There is plenty of room to walk your pets in the immediate area.

Drury Inn Denver East

4380 East Peoria Street 80239

303-373-1983 / 800-DRURYINN

> **Restaurant**: Short drive
>
> **H20**: Indoor/outdoor pool, outdoor hot tub
>
> **Pet Fee**: None
>
> **Refundable Pet Deposit**: None
>
> **Size Limit**: 50 lbs.
>
> **Terms**: Pets cannot be left unattended in the room.
>
> **Pet Amenities**: There is an open field next to the building to walk your dog.

Four Points by Sheraton Cherry Creek

600 South Colorado Blvd. 80246

303-757-3341 / 800-325-3535

> **Restaurant**: Boulevard Bistro
>
> **H20**: Seasonal outdoor pool
>
> **Pet Fee**: $25 per pet per stay
>
> **Refundable Pet Deposit**: None
>
> **Size Limit**: 50 lbs.
>
> **Terms**: Pets cannot be left unattended in room unless crated.
>
> **Pet Amenities**: Property is located on walking path along Cherry Creek.

Marriott TownePlace Suites...
A Place For You & Your
Furry Friends To Call Home!

An all suite hotel offering studio, one and two-bedroom suites, fully equipped kitchens, complimentary high-speed internet available in all suites, exercise facility, free local calls, seasonal outdoor pool (except downtown), 24-hour front desk, and free morning paper that your pet will only have to go to your front door to fetch.

7 Great Locations!

Broomfield/Boulder
(303) 466-2200

Downtown Denver
(303) 722-2322

Colorado Springs
(719) 594-4447

Littleton/Southwest
(303) 972-0555

Denver Southeast
(303) 759-9393

Denver Tech Center
(720) 875-1113

Lakewood
(303) 232-7790

Four Points by Sheraton Denver Southeast
6363 East Hampden Avenue 80222
303-758-7000 / 800-325-3535

> **Restaurant**: Westview Grill, The Lodge
>
> **H20**: Indoor pool and hot tub, seasonal outdoor pool
>
> **Pet Fee**: None
>
> **Refundable Pet Deposit**: None
>
> **Size Limit**: None
>
> **Terms**: Must sign pet policy agreement form.
>
> **Pet Amenities**: Grassy areas to walk pets on property.

Hampton Inn & Suites Denver Tech Center
5001 South Ulster Street 80237
303-804-9900 / 800-HAMPTON

> **Restaurant**: Walking distance
>
> **H20**: Outdoor hot tub, seasonal outdoor pool
>
> **Pet Fee**: None
>
> **Refundable Pet Deposit**: $20
>
> **Size Limit**: None
>
> **Terms**: Deposit is refundable after housekeeping inspection. Pets cannot be left unattended unless crated.
>
> **Pet Amenities**: There is a designated area to walk pets on property.

Hampton Inn Denver International Airport
6290 Tower Road 80249
303-371-0200 / 800-426-7866

> **Restaurant**: Walking distance
>
> **H20**: Indoor pool
>
> **Pet Fee**: None
>
> **Refundable Pet Deposit**: None
>
> **Size Limit**: None
>
> **Terms**: Pet rooms are on the first floor.
>
> **Pet Amenities**: Plenty of grassy areas to walk pets on property.

"In dog years, I'm dead."

-Unknown

Holiday Chalet Victorian B&B
1820 East Colfax Avenue 80218
303-321-9975 / 800-626-4497

Restaurant: Walking distance

H20: None

Pet Fee: None

Refundable Pet Deposit: None

Size Limit: None

Terms: Well-mannered dogs only. Pets cannot be left alone in rooms.

Pet Amenities: Dog loving staff! Resident dog to play with.
Cheesman Park is only two blocks away.

Holiday Inn - Denver Central
4849 Bannock Street 80216
303-292-9500 / 800-HOLIDAY

Restaurant: Teddy's

H20: Year round outdoor pool and hot tub

Pet Fee: None

Refundable Pet Deposit: $200

Size Limit: 45 lbs.

Terms: Well-behaved pets welcome.

Pet Amenities: There is a park nearby to walk pets.

Homestead Studio Suites Hotel
Denver Tech Center
4885 South Quebec Street 80237
303-689-9443 / 888-782-9473

Restaurant: Several within walking distance.

H20: None

Pet Fee: $25 per night up to $75 per stay

Refundable Pet Deposit: None

Size Limit: None

Terms: Well-behaved pets welcome.

Pet Amenities: Grassy areas on property to walk pets.

"A dog a day keeps the doctor away."
-Norman LaBlanc

"Best Place to Rest Weary Feet – and Paws"

— Westword 2002

Loews Denver Hotel offers personalized service and gorgeous accommodations for you and your furry friends.

Enjoy our 183 oversized guest rooms, Tuscany Restaurant, complimentary fitness center, parking and shuttle service to the Cherry Creek Shopping District.

Our **Loews Loves Pets** program includes:

- **Pet welcome amenity with welcome note from our GM**
- **Bark goodie bag with: Loews Hotels pet mat, bowl and treats**
- **Pet pagers available at the front desk**
- **Pet room service menu**
- **Our concierge offers complimentary pet walking, a list of vets, pet shops/groomers, pet sitters and pet friendly restaurants**
- **Deposits not required**

LOEWS DENVER HOTEL

4150 EAST MISSISSIPPI AVE, DENVER, CO 80246
303-782-9300 • 800-345-9172

Official Sponsor of Dumb Friends League Furry Scurry

The Hotel Monaco Denver
1717 Champa Street 80202
303-296-1717 / 800-397-5380

Restaurant: Panzano

H20: None

Pet Fee: None

Refundable Pet Deposit: None

Size Limit: None

Terms: Well-behaved pets are welcome.

Pet Amenities: Dog treats, food and water bowls on a mat, pet mitt, an information card which lists the best places to walk your dog near the hotel. Pet walking services are available.

Fido's Favorite Features: Ideal location, wonderful bedding, exceptional bath products, Renaissance Aveda Spa and Panzano. This impressive downtown hotel has a very stylish flair.

*Remington & Friends offers yummy gourmet treats, pet supplies, full service grooming and even scrumptious birthday cakes for your pet! While in Washington Park area, be sure to drop by for some fresh baked goodies, Fido will thank you.

The Hotel Teatro
1100 14th Street 80202
303-228-1100 / 888-727-1200

Restaurant: Kevin Taylor, Restaurant Prima

H20: None

Pet Fee: None

Refundable Pet Deposit: None

Size Limit: None

Terms: Well-behaved pets are welcome.

Pet Amenities: Silver water and food bowls which are tagged with pet's name, chilled bottled water, assortment of treats. Your pet also receives a handsome identification tag with the hotel's information engraved. There is a nice walking path one block from the hotel.

Fido's Favorite Features: Immaculate, spacious and plush accommodations, pet-friendly staff, both restaurants. This impressive hotel offers nothing less than a top-notch experience.

JW Marriott Denver at Cherry Creek
150 Clayton Lane 80206
303-316-2700 / 800-228-9290

> **Restaurant**: Mirepoix
>
> **H20**: Two outdoor hot tubs
>
> **Pet Fee**: None
>
> **Refundable Pet Deposit**: None
>
> **Size Limit**: None
>
> **Terms**: Pets cannot be left in room unattended. Pets must be leashed while in common areas.
>
> **Pet Amenities**: Biscuits at check in. The doorman usually has bottomless pockets of treats. There are grassy areas nearby for walking your pets.
>
> **Fido's Favorite Features**: Mirepoix, prime location, gorgeous accommodations. This fine hotel is very pet-friendly and sure to please both you and Fido!
>
> *CB Paws is Cherry Creek's posh pet boutique. You can walk your dog down to pick out some gourmet treats, fine accessories, pet furniture and more.

La Quinta Inn & Suites
Denver International Airport
6801 Tower Rd. 80249
303-371-0888 / 800-531-5900

Restaurant: Walking distance

H20: Indoor pool and hot tub

Pet Fee: None

Refundable Pet Deposit: None

Size Limit: None

Terms: Pets cannot be left unattended in room.

Pet Amenities: Doggie welcome bags at check in. Large courtyard to walk your pets.

La Quinta Inn Denver Central
3500 Park Avenue West 80216
303-458-1222 / 800-531-5900

Restaurant: Within walking distance.

H20: Seasonal outdoor pool

Pet Fee: None

Refundable Pet Deposit: None

Size Limit: None

Terms: Pets cannot be left unattended in room.

Pet Amenities: There is a grassy area to walk your pet on property.

Traveling With Your Pet ...In Style!

La Quinta Inn Denver
1975 South Colorado Blvd. 80222
303-758-8886 / 800-531-5900

> **Restaurant**: Walking distance to several restaurants.
>
> **H20**: Seasonal outdoor pool
>
> **Pet Fee**: None
>
> **Refundable Pet Deposit**: None
>
> **Size Limit**: None
>
> **Terms**: Pets cannot be left unattended in room.
>
> **Pet Amenities**: There is a grassy area to walk your pet.

Loews Denver Hotel
4150 East Mississippi Avenue 80246
303-782-9300 / 800-345-9172

> **Restaurant**: Tuscany
>
> **H20**: None
>
> **Pet Fee**: None
>
> **Refundable Pet Deposit**: None
>
> **Size Limit**: None
>
> **Terms**: Well-behaved pets are welcome.
>
> **Pet Amenities**: Pet welcome bag at check in includes gourmet treats, a dog dish with floor mat and a Loews logo lid for canned food. Gourmet pet room service available! See Concierge for a list of local pet-friendly services and businesses. Complimentary pet walking services available. Pet pagers are available upon request. Ample pet walking area. Nice grassy area behind hotel to walk pets. Look for the pet pick up station.
>
> **Fido's Favorite Features**: The superior accommodations, Tuscany, pet welcome bag, flower gardens and grassy area in back by pet area. The liberal and convenient pet policy. The Loews Hotel is an elegant property which is sure to please you and Fido of course.
>
> * When it's time for your pooch to hit the doggie spa, be sure to check out Vanity Fur, a fantastic local pet boutique and doggie spa.

"I once decided not to date a guy because he wasn't excited to meet my dog. I mean, this was like not wanting to meet my mother."

-Bonnie Schacter

You stay in bed.
We'll walk the dog.

It's a beautiful relationship with only one problem - you like to sleep in and she likes to go for early morning walks. Get a new leash on life at the Hotel Monaco. Treats to tricks, we'll take care of your girl. Not to mention you.

HOTEL MONACO
DENVER

1717 Champa at 17th Street
Denver, CO 80202

800.397.5380
303.296.1717
MONACO-DENVER.COM

KIMPTON BOUTIQUE HOTELS

Magnolia Hotel Denver
818 17th Street 80202
303-607-9000 / 888-915-1110

> **Restaurant**: Harry's
>
> **H20**: None
>
> **Pet Fee**: $10 per night per pet
>
> **Refundable Pet Deposit**: None
>
> **Size Limit**: None
>
> **Terms**: Well-behaved pets welcome. Guest is responsible for damage caused by pets.
>
> **Pet Amenities**: Pet walking services available upon request. Extremely pet friendly staff. There are grassy areas and nearby parks for walking your dog.
>
> **Fido's Favorite Features**: Stylish accommodations, wonderful bedding, over-sized bathtubs. Harry's, pet friendly staff, great location. The Magnolia Hotel offers a nice included expanded breakfast and complimentary fresh baked cookies in the evening. This fine hotel pays attention to every detail.
>
> * A Pet's Paradise is not a far drive, they will provide your pet with the most healthful treats, food and supplies imaginable. Your pet will thank you!

Radisson Hotel Denver Stapleton Plaza
3333 Quebec Street 80207
303-321-3500 / 800-333-3333

> **Restaurant**: Quebec's Bistro
>
> **H20**: Seasonal outdoor pool and indoor hot tub.
>
> **Pet Fee**: $25 per room per stay
>
> **Refundable Pet Deposit**: None
>
> **Size Limit**: None
>
> **Terms**: Pets cannot be left unattended in room.
>
> **Pet Amenities**: There is ample space on property to walk pets.

"If dogs could talk it would take a lot of fun out of owning one."

-Andy Rooney

Ramada Continental Hotel
2601 Zuni Street 80211
303-433-6677 / 800-2RAMADA
> **Restaurant**: The Board Room, Club 212
> **H20**: Seasonal outdoor pool
> **Pet Fee**: $20 per stay per room
> **Refundable Pet Deposit**: None
> **Size Limit**: None
> **Terms**: Well-behaved pets welcome. Must register pets at check in.
> **Pet Amenities**: There is a large park down the street to walk pets.

Ramada Limited & Suites
7020 Tower Road 80249
303-373-1600 / 800-2RAMADA
> **Restaurant**: Walking distance
> **H20**: Indoor pool and hot tub
> **Pet Fee**: $35 per room per stay
> **Refundable Pet Deposit**: None
> **Size Limit**: None
> **Terms**: Pets cannot be left in room unattended.
> **Pet Amenities**: There is a big field next to the hotel to walk pets.

Red Lion Hotel - Denver Central
4040 Quebec Street 80216
303-321-6666 / 800-RED-LION
> **Restaurant**: Amberstone Grille
> **H20**: Seasonal outdoor pool
> **Pet Fee**: $25 per stay per room
> **Refundable Pet Deposit**: None
> **Size Limit**: None
> **Terms**: Pet rooms are located on the first floor and are all smoking rooms.
> **Pet Amenities**: Plenty of grassy areas around property to walk your dog.

Red Lion Hotel Denver
Downtown at Invesco Field
1975 Bryant Street 80204
303-433-8331 / 800-RED-LION

Restaurant: Skybox Bar and Grill

H20: Seasonal outdoor pool

Pet Fee: None

Refundable Pet Deposit: $50

Size Limit: None

Terms: Well-behaved pets only.

Pet Amenities: Plenty of grassy areas around property to walk your dogs.

Red Roof Inn & Suites
Denver International Airport
6890 Tower Rd. 80249
303-371-5300 / 800-RED-ROOF

Restaurant: Walking distance

H20: Indoor pool and hot tub

Pet Fee: None

Refundable Pet Deposit: None

Size Limit: None

Terms: Pets cannot be left in the room unattended.

Pet Amenities: Treats at check in. Ample space to walk your dogs on property.

Residence Inn Downtown
2777 Zuni Street 80211
303-458-5318 / 800-331-3131

> **Restaurant**: Short drive
>
> **H20**: Outdoor hot tub, seasonal outdoor pool
>
> **Pet Fee**: $75 one time fee per room
>
> **Refundable Pet Deposit**: None
>
> **Size Limit**: None
>
> **Terms**: Well-behaved pets are welcome. Guest is responsible for any damaged caused by pets.
>
> **Pet Amenities**: Pet relief areas are located on both the north and south sides of the property. Just a few blocks away, there are grassy areas, parks and a bike path running along the creek.

"Some of my best leading men have been dogs and horses."
-Elizabeth Taylor

Staybridge Suites

4220 East Virginia Avenue 80246

303-321-5757 / 800-HOLIDAY

> **Restaurant**: Within walking distance
>
> **H20**: Seasonal outdoor hot tub
>
> **Pet Fee**: $75 per room for entire stay
>
> **Refundable Pet Deposit**: None
>
> **Size Limit**: 50 lbs.
>
> **Terms**: Two pets per room maximum. Cats must be declawed.
>
> **Pet Amenities**: There is a walking path along Cherry Creek located in front of the hotel. Pet pick up station located at grassy pet walk area.
>
> **Fido's Favorite Features**: Convenient walking path along property, easy access to Cherry Creek Shopping District, comfortable accommodations.

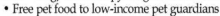

TownePlace Suites by Marriott
Denver Southeast

3699 S. Monaco Pkwy 80237

303-759-9393 / 800-257-3000

Restaurant: Walking distance

H20: Seasonal outdoor pool

Pet Fee: $25 per day/ $200 maximum per stay

Refundable Pet Deposit: None

Size Limit: None

Terms: Pets must be house trained and well-behaved.

Pet Amenities: Pet walking area on property. Pet treats at check in. Flexible housekeeping to accommodate guest's schedule with pets.

"No matter how little money and how few possessions you own, having a dog makes you rich."

-Louis Sabin

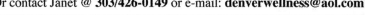

TownePlace Suites by Marriott - Downtown
685 Speer Boulevard 80204
303-722-2322 / 800-257-3000

> **Restaurant**: Walking distance
>
> **H20**: None
>
> **Pet Fee**: $20 per day / $200 maximum per stay
>
> **Refundable Pet Deposit**: None
>
> **Size Limit**: None
>
> **Terms**: Pets must be house trained and well-behaved.
>
> **Pet Amenities**: Pet walking area on property. Pet treats at check in. Flexible housekeeping to accommodate guest's schedule with pets. Sunken Gardens Park is two blocks north for exercising pets.

The Warwick Hotel- Denver
1776 Grant Street 80203
303-861-2000 / 800-525-2888

> **Restaurant**: Randolph's Bar & Restaurant
>
> **H20**: Year round outdoor pool
>
> **Pet Fee**: None
>
> **Refundable Pet Deposit**: $200
>
> **Size Limit**: None
>
> **Terms**: Well-behaved dogs welcome. No cats allowed.
>
> **Pet Amenities**: Treats and pet dishes at check in. There is plenty of room to walk pets near property.
>
> **Fido's Favorite Features**: Pet-friendly staff, Randolph's, rooftop year round heated pool.

Pocky Wark

The Westin Tabor Center

1672 Lawrence Street 80202

303-572-9100 / 888-627-8435

> **Restaurant**: Augusta, The Palm
>
> **H20**: Indoor / Outdoor pool, outdoor hot tub
>
> **Pet Fee**: None
>
> **Refundable Pet Deposit**: None
>
> **Size Limit**: 40 lbs.
>
> **Terms**: Must make arrangements with housekeeping or pet must be crated for housekeeping to enter room.
>
> **Pet Amenities**: Skyline Park is located behind the hotel, walking path along creek nearby.
>
> **Fido's Favorite Features**: The heavenly beds, double showerheads, the spacious rooms, nice pool area, ideal location.
>
> * Be sure to walk Fido down to Colorado Petfitters' riverside location for healthy treats, toys and some fun in the park.

-Dillon-

Best Western Ptarmigan Lodge

652 Lake Dillon Drive 80435

970-468-2341 / 800-842-5939

> **Restaurant**: Walking distance
>
> **H20**: Indoor hot tub
>
> **Pet Fee**: $15 per stay per pet
>
> **Refundable Pet Deposit**: None
>
> **Size Limit**: None
>
> **Terms**: Call the front desk to arrange housekeeping. If your pet is left unattended in room, it must be crated.
>
> **Pet Amenities**: Lake Dillon is conveniently located across the street for your pet's swimming pleasure. There is also ample space for your dogs to run.

"A piece of grass a day, keeps the Vet away."
-Unknown dog

Dillon Super 8
808 Little Beaver Trail 80435
970-468-8888 / 800-800-8000

>**Restaurant**: Several within walking distance.
>
>**H20**: None
>
>**Pet Fee**: $15 per pet per stay
>
>**Refundable Pet Deposit**: None
>
>**Size Limit**: None
>
>**Terms**: Pets cannot be left in room unattended.
>
>**Pet Amenities**: There is plenty of grass to walk your pet on property.

-Durango-

Alpine Inn
3515 North Main Avenue 81301
970-247-4042 / 800-818-4042

>**Restaurant**: Within walking distance
>
>**H20**: None
>
>**Pet Fee**: $5 per room per night
>
>**Refundable Pet Deposit**: None
>
>**Size Limit**: None
>
>**Terms**: Pets cannot be left in room unattended.
>
>**Pet Amenities**: There are areas to walk your pets on property.

Comfort Inn
2930 North Main Avenue 81301
970-259-5373 / 800-532-7112

>**Restaurant**: Several within walking distance
>
>**H20**: Seasonal outdoor pool, two indoor hot tubs.
>
>**Pet Fee**: $10 per room per stay
>
>**Refundable Pet Deposit**: None
>
>**Size Limit**: 50 lbs.
>
>**Terms**: Pets cannot be left in room unattended.
>
>**Pet Amenities**: There is a walking path to the river behind the property.

Doubletree Hotel Durango

501 Camino Del Rio 81301

970-259-6580 / 800-222-TREE

Restaurant: Edgewater Restaurant and Lounge

H20: Indoor pool and hot tub

Pet Fee: $15 per day per room

Refundable Pet Deposit: $50 cash or credit card

Size Limit: None

Terms: Pets cannot be left unattended in room.

Pet Amenities: The River Walk is located behind the property and there is a nearby park for walking your dog.

Fido's Favorite Features: Accommodating staff, comfortable beds, nice lobby area. Your pooch will love the River Walk behind the hotel. Leash-free park is a short walk.

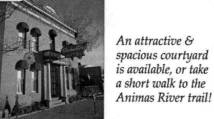

Holiday Inn Durango
800 Camino Del Rio 81301
970-247-5393 / 800-HOLIDAY

Restaurant: Applebee's

H20: Indoor pool and hot tub

Pet Fee: $10 per day per pet

Refundable Pet Deposit: None

Size Limit: None

Terms: Well-behaved pets only.

Pet Amenities: River Walk is located behind the property, and there is also a nearby park to walk your pets.

The Inn at Durango Mountain
49617 US 550 North 81301
970-247-9669 / 800-678-1000

Restaurant: Hamilton's Chop House

H20: Indoor pool and hot tub

Pet Fee: $10 per day per pet

Refundable Pet Deposit: None

Size Limit: None

Terms: Pets cannot be left in room unattended.

Pet Amenities: There is ample space to walk pets.

Iron Horse Inn
5800 N. Main Avenue 81301
970-259-1010 / 800-748-2990

Restaurant: Walking distance

H20: Indoor pool and hot tub

Pet Fee: None

Refundable Pet Deposit: None

Size Limit: None

Terms: Pets cannot be left in room unattended at any time.

Pet Amenities: There is plenty of space for pets to run on property.

Quality Inn & Suites

455 S. Camino Del Rio 81301
970-259-7900 / 888-259-7903

> **Restaurant**: Walking distance
>
> **H20**: Indoor pool and hot tub
>
> **Pet Fee**: $10 per night per room
>
> **Refundable Pet Deposit**: None
>
> **Size Limit**: None
>
> **Terms**: Pets cannot be left in room unattended. Pet rooms are on the first and second floors only.
>
> **Pet Amenities**: There is a grassy area in front of the hotel to walk your dog.

Residence Inn

21691 Highway 160 West 81301
970-259-6200 / 800-331-3131

> **Restaurant**: Walking distance
>
> **H20**: Indoor pool and hot tub
>
> **Pet Fee**: $75 per stay
>
> **Refundable Pet Deposit**: None
>
> **Size Limit**: 35 lbs.
>
> **Terms**: Well-behaved pets only. Pets cannot be left in room unattended.
>
> **Pet Amenities**: Located three blocks from River Walk.

Rather than your home phone number, use your cell phone number for your pet's Identification tags.

The Rochester Hotel
721 East Second Avenue 81301
970-385-1920 / 800-664-1920

Restaurant: Walking distance

H20: None

Pet Fee: $20 per day per pet

Refundable Pet Deposit: None

Size Limit: None

Terms: Must sign pet agreement form upon check in. Pets cannot be left unattended in room and are not allowed on the furniture. Guest must pick up after pets. Guest is responsible for damages.

Pet Amenities: Well-behaved pets are welcome. A pet bed and treats will be waiting for your pet. There are grassy areas to walk your dog near the hotel.

Fido's Favorite Features: A wonderful gourmet breakfast is included, tasteful old west decor, convenient yet quiet location.
This stylish hotel has a very friendly and accommodating staff.

Travelodge
2970 Main Avenue 81301
970-247-1741 / 800-578-7878

Restaurant: Within walking distance

H20: Outdoor hot tub

Pet Fee: $5 per day for small dogs / $8 per day for large dogs

Refundable Pet Deposit: None

Size Limit: None

Terms: Well-behaved pets welcome.

Pet Amenities: The river is located behind the property. There is plenty of room for your pet to run.

"Dogs laugh, but they laugh with their tails."
-Max Eastman

-Eagle-

Americinn Lodge & Suites
85 Pond Road 81631
970-328-5155 / 800-634-3444

> **Restaurant**: Short drive
>
> **H20**: Indoor pool and hot tub
>
> **Pet Fee**: $25 per stay per room
>
> **Refundable Pet Deposit**: None
>
> **Size Limit**: None
>
> **Terms**: Well-behaved pets only.
>
> **Pet Amenities**: There is plenty of space to walk dogs on the property.

Best Western Eagle Lodge & Suites
200 Loren Lane 81631
970-328-6316 / 800-SKI-VAIL

> **Restaurant**: Several within walking distance
>
> **H20**: Indoor pool and hot tub
>
> **Pet Fee**: $10 per night per pet
>
> **Refundable Pet Deposit**: $50
>
> **Size Limit**: None
>
> **Terms**: Guest is responsible for damages caused by pet. Deposit is refunded after housekeeping inspection.
>
> **Pet Amenities**: There are grassy areas to walk pets around the lodge.

Holiday Inn Express
75 Pond Road 81631
970-328-8088 / 888-30-EAGLE

> **Restaurant**: Within walking distance
>
> **H20**: Indoor pool and hot tub
>
> **Pet Fee**: $20 per stay per room
>
> **Refundable Pet Deposit**: None
>
> **Size Limit**: None
>
> **Terms**: Pets cannot be left unattended in room.
>
> **Pet Amenities**: Pet exercise area on property.

-Edwards-

Inn & Suites at Riverwalk
27 Main Street 81632
970-926-0606 / 888-926-0606

Restaurant: Full Belly Kitchen & Pub, Frites

H20: Year round outdoor pool and hot tub

Pet Fee: $25 per pet per stay

Refundable Pet Deposit: None

Size Limit: None

Terms: Well-behaved pets welcome.

Pet Amenities: Ample walking area located behind the hotel.

Fido's Favorite Features: Stylish accommodations, beautiful lobby, nice pool area, pet friendly staff. This fantastic property is conveniently located near I-70.

* Be sure to drop into local store, The Pet Spot. They carry quality foods, treats and other great products for Fido.

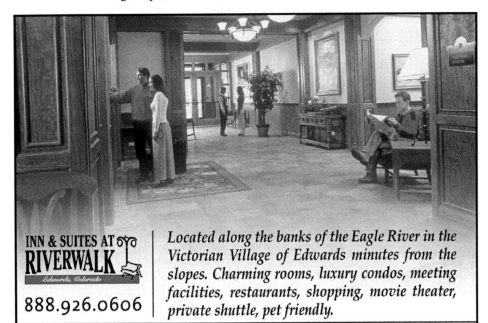

-Englewood-

Amerisuites Denver Tech Center
8300 E. Crescent Pkwy 80111
303-804-0700 / 800-833-1516

Restaurant: Walking distance

H20: Indoor pool

Pet Fee: $10 per day per pet

Refundable Pet Deposit: None

Size Limit: 60 lbs.

Terms: Well-behaved pets only.

Pet Amenities: There are plenty of grassy areas around the property for walking dogs.

*Paw Prints is a wonderful healthy pet supply store, guaranteed to make Fido feel like a King. Be sure to check it out while visiting Englewood.

"I spilled spot remover on my dog. He's gone now."
-Steven Wright

Best Western Denver Tech Center

9799 East Geddes 80112

303-768-9300 / 800-WESTERN

Restaurant: Several within walking distance

H20: Indoor pool and hot tub

Pet Fee: $25 per room per stay

Refundable Pet Deposit: None

Size Limit: None

Terms: Pets must be well-behaved.

Pet Amenities: There is ample space to walk your pets on property.

Drury Inn & Suites Denver Tech Center

9445 E. Dry Creek Rd. 80112

303-694-3400 / 800-DRURYINN

Restaurant: Short drive

H20: Year round indoor / outdoor pool and indoor hot tub

Pet Fee: None

Refundable Pet Deposit: None

Size Limit: None

Terms: Must sign pet policy agreement at check in. Pets cannot be left unattended in room.

Pet Amenities: Dog biscuits at front desk. Grassy areas around property to walk your dog.

Hampton Inn Denver Southeast

9231 E. Arapahoe Rd. 80112

303-792-9999 / 800-HAMPTON

Restaurant: Walking distance

H20: Seasonal outdoor pool

Pet Fee: $10 per night per pet

Refundable Pet Deposit: None

Size Limit: None

Terms: None

Pet Amenities: Dog treats at check in.

Quality Suites 🐾 🐾 🐾
7374 South Clinton Street 80112
303-858-0700 / 800-4CHOICE

Restaurant: Several within walking distance.

H20: Indoor pool and hot tub

Pet Fee: $50 per stay per room

Refundable Pet Deposit: None

Size Limit: None

Terms: Well-behaved pets welcome.

Pet Amenities: Grassy area behind hotel for walking pets.

Residence Inn Denver Tech Center
6565 S. Yosemite Street 80111
303-740-7177 / 800-331-3131

> **Restaurant**: Several within walking distance.
>
> **H20**: Outdoor hot tub, seasonal outdoor pool
>
> **Pet Fee**: $75 one time fee per stay per room
>
> **Refundable Pet Deposit**: None
>
> **Size Limit**: None
>
> **Terms**: Maximum of two dogs per room.
>
> **Pet Amenities**: Dog walk / run on property

Residence Inn Denver South
8322 S. Valley Highway 80112
720-895-0200 / 800-331-3131

> **Restaurant**: Short drive
>
> **H20**: Indoor pool and hot tub
>
> **Pet Fee**: $75 per stay per room
>
> **Refundable Pet Deposit**: None
>
> **Size Limit**: None
>
> **Terms**: Guest is responsible for damage caused by pets.
>
> **Pet Amenities**: Grassy areas on property for walking dogs.

TownePlace Suites by Marriott Denver Tech Center
7877 S. Chester Street 80112
720-875-1113 / 800-257-3000

> **Restaurant**: Short drive
>
> **H20**: Seasonal outdoor pool
>
> **Pet Fee**: $25 per night, $75 maximum per stay
>
> **Refundable Pet Deposit**: None
>
> **Size Limit**: None
>
> **Terms**: Pets must be house trained and well-behaved.
>
> **Pet Amenities**: Pet walking area on property. Pet treats at check in. Flexible housekeeping to accommodate guest's schedule with pets.
>
> * When in Englewood, Rocky Mountain Paw Pourri is a must for pet lovers. They carry unique gifts, wholesome treats and many other items to tempt your pooch.

-Estes Park-

Budget Host Four Winds Motor Lodge
1120 Big Thompson Avenue 80517
970-586-3313 / 800-527-7509

> **Restaurant**: Short drive
>
> **H20**: Seasonal outdoor pool, indoor hot tub
>
> **Pet Fee**: $15 per pet per night
>
> **Refundable Pet Deposit**: None
>
> **Size Limit**: 25 lbs.
>
> **Terms**: Cannot walk pets on property. Pets cannot be left in room unattended.
>
> **Pet Amenities**: There is a dog park nearby to run your dogs.

Castle Mountain Lodge
1520 Fall River Road 80517
970-586-3664 / 800-852-7463

> **Restaurant**: Walking distance
>
> **H20**: Indoor hot tub
>
> **Pet Fee**: $15 per night per pet
>
> **Refundable Pet Deposit**: None
>
> **Size Limit**: None
>
> **Terms**: 2 pets maximum. Well-behaved pets only.
>
> **Pet Amenities**: Short drive to Lake Estes, where there is a walking trail.

Holiday Inn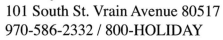
101 South St. Vrain Avenue 80517
970-586-2332 / 800-HOLIDAY

> **Restaurant**: JR Chapins
>
> **H20**: Indoor pool and hot tub
>
> **Pet Fee**: $10 per day per room
>
> **Refundable Pet Deposit**: None
>
> **Size Limit**: 100 lbs.
>
> **Terms**: Must sign pet policy at check in. Pets cannot be left unattended in room. Guest is responsible for damage caused by pets.
>
> **Pet Amenities**: Designated pet walking area on property.

Silver Moon Inn
175 Spruce Drive 80517
970-586-6006 / 800-818-6006

>**Restaurant**: Walking distance to several restaurants
>
>**H20**: Seasonal outdoor pool, two outdoor hot tubs.
>
>**Pet Fee**: None
>
>**Refundable Pet Deposit**: None
>
>**Size Limit**: None
>
>**Terms**: Well-behaved pets only. Barkers cannot be left in room alone.
>
>**Pet Amenities**: Plenty of space to walk pets on property. Fall River runs in front of the hotel property. Pet treats at check in.

The Stanley Hotel
333 Wonderview Avenue 80517
970-586-3371 / 800-976-1377

>**Restaurant**: Cascades
>
>**H20**: Seasonal outdoor pool
>
>**Pet Fee**: $100 per stay per room
>
>**Refundable Pet Deposit**: None
>
>**Size Limit**: None
>
>**Terms**: Pets must be crated if left unattended in room. Guest is responsible for damages caused by pets. Only one pet allowed per room.
>
>**Pet Amenities**: 20 acres to walk your dog.

-Evans-

Sleep Inn Greeley/Evans
3025 8th Avenue 80620
970-356-2180 / 800-424-6423

>**Restaurant**: Walking distance
>
>**H20**: Seasonal outdoor pool and hot tub
>
>**Pet Fee**: $15 per room per stay
>
>**Refundable Pet Deposit**: None
>
>**Size Limit**: None
>
>**Terms**: Pets cannot be left in room unattended.
>
>**Pet Amenities**: There is a designated pet walking area on property

-Evergreen-

Quality Suites
29300 U.S. Highway 40 80401
303-526-2000 / 800-4CHOICE

Restaurant: Walking distance

H20: Indoor pool and hot tub, two outdoor hot tubs

Pet Fee: None

Refundable Pet Deposit: $50

Size Limit: None

Terms: Pets cannot be left unattended in rooms. Well-behaved pets only.

Pet Amenities: Treats at check in. There is a private patio from pet rooms accessing grassy areas. Pet welcome bag at check in.

Fido's Favorite Features: Very pet-friendly staff, great pet welcome bag, nice expanded continental breakfast. This is an outstanding Quality Suites property!

Traveling With Your Pet ...In Style!

-Fairplay-

The Hand Hotel B&B
531 Front Street 80440
719-836-3595

>**Restaurant**: Walking distance
>**H20**: None
>**Pet Fee**: $5 per day per pet
>**Refundable Pet Deposit**: None
>**Size Limit**: None
>**Terms**: No more than three dogs per room. Well-behaved pets welcome.
>**Pet Amenities**: A walking path and a lake are located behind the hotel.

The Western Inn
490 Highway 285 80440
719-836-2026 / 877-306-3037

>**Restaurant**: Walking distance
>**H20**: Indoor hot tub
>**Pet Fee**: $5 per stay per room
>**Refundable Pet Deposit**: None
>**Size Limit**: None
>**Terms**: None
>**Pet Amenities**: There is an area to walk your dogs behind the building.

Salty Dog

-Fort Collins-

Armstrong Hotel
259 South College Avenue 80524
970-484-3883 / 866-384-3883

Restaurant: Several within the same block.

H20: None

Pet Fee: $15 per room for entire stay

Refundable Pet Deposit: None

Size Limit: None

Terms: Only three pet-friendly rooms available, call in advance. Pets cannot be left in room unattended.

Pet Amenities: Pet-friendly staff. Resident cat to keep Fido alert.

Best Western University Inn
914 South College Avenue 80524
970-484-1984 / 888-484-BWUI

Restaurant: Within walking distance of several

H20: Indoor pool and hot tub

Pet Fee: $10 per night per pet

Refundable Pet Deposit: None

Size Limit: None

Terms: Pet policy agreement form at check in. Well-behaved pets welcome.

Pet Amenities: Special rates for CSU Veterinary Hospital patients.

Comfort Suites
1415 Oakridge Drive 80525
970-206-4597 / 800-4CHOICE

Restaurant: Several within walking distance.

H20: Indoor hot tub and pool

Pet Fee: $15 per day per room

Refundable Pet Deposit: None

Size Limit: None

Terms: Well-behaved, quiet pets are welcome.

Pet Amenities: Ample pet walking area on property.

Consider Fort Collins

when planning your trip to Colorado!

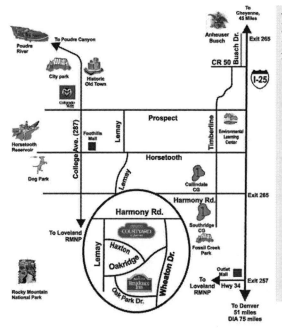

Fort Collins is centrally located and convenient to many activities:

- 1hour from Denver
- 45 min. from Estes Park
- Historic Old Town
- Colorado State University
- Local brewery tours
- Budweiser brewery tours
- Great local restaurants
- Rocky Mountain National park
- Poudre canyon park
- Fishing, hiking, biking, river rafting
- Many public golf courses

Red rover, Red rover, send your doggie right over.

Paws-itively the best hotel for you and your family. Wonderful walking trails near the hotel and plenty of outdoor adventure opportunities in the area Off-leash Dog Park close by. Recognized by Family Circle Magazine as a pet-friendly paradise
Doggie treats included!

1127 Oakridge Drive
Reservations : 800-331-3131

Spacious studio, one and two bedroom suites with fully equipped kitchens. Complimentary daily hot breakfast buffet and evening social Mon-Thurs. Fitness room, indoor pool and whirlpool.

Courtyard by Marriott

1200 Oakridge Drive 80525
970-282-1700 / 800-321-2211

>**Restaurant**: Several within walking distance
>
>**H20**: Indoor pool or hot tub
>
>**Pet Fee**: $25 for one night, two to four $50 , five or more $75
>
>**Refundable Pet Deposit**: None
>
>**Size Limit**: Prefer smaller pets.
>
>**Terms**: Pets cannot be left in room unattended unless crated.
>
>**Pet Amenities**: Plenty of space to walk pets on property and in the area.

Fort Collins Marriott

350 Horsetooth Road 80525
970-226-5200 / 800-548-2635

>**Restaurant**: The Copper Creek, The Falls Lounge
>
>**H20**: Indoor / outdoor pool (outdoor portion seasonal), indoor hot tub
>
>**Pet Fee**: $10 per night per pet
>
>**Refundable Pet Deposit**: None
>
>**Size Limit**: None
>
>**Terms**: Make arrangements with housekeeping to have room serviced if pet is not crated. Pets must be leashed in all common areas.
>
>**Pet Amenities**: There is plenty of space to walk your pets on property. A park and walking trails are within walking distance of the hotel.
>
>**Fido's Favorite Features**: Comfortable and spacious rooms, convenient access to walking trails for pet exercise. This full service hotel's staff is very friendly and accommodating.

 **During warm or cold months, NEVER leave your pet in the car, even for a short period of time.**

Hampton Inn
1620 Oakridge Drive 80525
970-229-5927 / 800-HAMPTON

    Restaurant: Walking distance

    H20: Indoor pool and hot tub

    Pet Fee: $25 per pet per stay

    Refundable Pet Deposit: None

    Size Limit: None

    Terms: Pets cannot be left unattended in room.

    Pet Amenities: Pet walking areas on property.

Hilton Fort Collins
425 West Prospect Road 80526
970-482-2626 / 800-HILTONS

    Restaurant: The Park, The Court

    H20: Indoor pool and hot tub

    Pet Fee: $25 per room per stay

    Refundable Pet Deposit: None

    Size Limit: None

    Terms: Well-behaved pets welcome

    Pet Amenities: Plenty of room to walk pets behind hotel.

    Fido's Favorite Features: Nice lobby area, convenient location to CSU, stylish accommodations.

The Plaza Inn
3907 East Mulberry 80524
970-493-7800 / 800-434-5548

    Restaurant: Bruno's

    H20: Indoor pool and hot tub, seasonal outdoor pool

    Pet Fee: $5 per day per pet

    Refundable Pet Deposit: None

    Size Limit: None

    Terms: Pets cannot be left in room unattended.

    Pet Amenities: There is space to walk pets behind the property.

Quality Inn & Suites

4001 S. Mason Street 80525

970-282-9047 / 800-228-5151

Restaurant: Short drive

H20: Indoor pool and hot tub

Pet Fee: None

Refundable Pet Deposit: None

Size Limit: None

Terms: $100 fee for undeclared pets. Pet rooms are on the first floor only.

Pet Amenities: There is plenty of room to walk pets on property.

Ramada Fort Collins

3836 East Mulberry 80524

970-484-4660 / 800-2RAMADA

Restaurant: US Bar & Grill

H20: Indoor pool and hot tub

Pet Fee: $30 per room per stay

Refundable Pet Deposit: None

Size Limit: None

Terms: Two pets per room maximum.

Pet Amenities: Pets cannot be left in room unattended.

"Every dog isn't a growler and every growler isn't a dog."

-Anonymous

Residence Inn

1127 Oakridge Drive 80525

970-223-5700 / 800-331-3131

> **Restaurant**: Walking distance
>
> **H20**: Indoor pool and hot tub
>
> **Pet Fee**: $75 per room per stay
>
> **Refundable Pet Deposit**: None
>
> **Size Limit**: None
>
> **Terms**: Guest is responsible for pet's behavior.
>
> **Pet Amenities**: Welcome treats await your pet at the front desk. If your pet is sick and visiting the CSU Teaching Veterinary Hospital, the hotel staff offers a wellness basket. Ample dog walking areas on property.
>
> **Fido's Favorite Features**: The pet friendly staff really takes the extra step to make sure that both you and your pet have a comfortable stay. This exceptional Residence Inn is sure to please.
>
> * If you are busy with business or an activity where Fido isn't welcome, take your pooch to Dapper Dog Salon for a vacation of his own.

Sleep Inn

3808 East Mulberry 80524

970-484-5515 / 800-4CHOICE

> **Restaurant**: Several within walking distance.
>
> **H20**: None
>
> **Pet Fee**: $10 per pet per stay
>
> **Refundable Pet Deposit**: None
>
> **Size Limit**: None
>
> **Terms**: Well-behaved pets only.
>
> **Pet Amenities**: Grassy area on property for walking pets.

"In order to really enjoy a dog, one doesn't merely try to train him to be semi-human. The point of it is to open oneself to the possibility of becoming partly a dog."
                                              -Edward Hoagland

Super 8 Motel 🐾
409 Centro Way 80524
970-493-7701 / 800-800-8000

> **Restaurant**: Several within walking distance.
>
> **H20**: Indoor hot tub
>
> **Pet Fee**: $5 per pet per day
>
> **Refundable Pet Deposit**: None
>
> **Size Limit**: None
>
> **Terms**: Pet policy form at check in. Pets cannot be left in room unattended. Pets are not allowed on bed. Owner is responsible for pet's behavior.
>
> **Pet Amenities**: Pet walking area near property.

-Fort Morgan-

Affordable Inns 🐾
1409 Barlow Road 80701
970-867-9481 / 877-906-0412

> **Restaurant**: Maverick's Country Grill
>
> **H20**: Seasonal outdoor pool and hot tub
>
> **Pet Fee**: $10 per room per day
>
> **Refundable Pet Deposit**: None
>
> **Size Limit**: None
>
> **Terms**: Well-behaved pets only.
>
> **Pet Amenities**: There is ample space for walking pets.

Best Western Park Terrace Inn
725 Main Street 80701
970-867-8256 / 888-593-5793

> **Restaurant**: Memories
>
> **H20**: Outdoor hot tub, seasonal outdoor pool
>
> **Pet Fee**: $10 per stay per pet
>
> **Refundable Pet Deposit**: None
>
> **Size Limit**: None
>
> **Terms**: Guest is responsible for damage caused by pets.
>
> **Pet Amenities**: City parks and walking trails are a few blocks away.

-Frisco-

Best Western Lake Dillon Lodge
1202 Summit Boulevard 80443
970-668-5094 / 800-727-0607

> **Restaurant**: Casey's
>
> **H20**: Indoor pool and two hot tubs
>
> **Pet Fee**: $15 per room per stay
>
> **Refundable Pet Deposit**: None
>
> **Size Limit**: None
>
> **Terms**: Must occupy a smoking room.
>
> **Pet Amenities**: Ample pet walking area on property. Lake Dillon is a short distance from the lodge.

Holiday Inn Summit County
1129 N. Summit Boulevard 80443
970-668-5000 / 800-782-7669

> **Restaurant**: Frisco City Limits, Holiday Bistro
>
> **H20**: Indoor pool and two hot tubs
>
> **Pet Fee**: $20 per room per stay
>
> **Refundable Pet Deposit**: None
>
> **Size Limit**: None
>
> **Terms**: Must sign pet policy agreement upon check in. Pet rooms are on the first floor and are smoking rooms. Barkers cannot be left unattended in room.
>
> **Pet Amenities**: Lake Dillon is a short walk. There is plenty of room for your pet to run and swim.

Hotel Frisco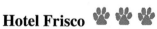
308 Main Street 80443
970-668-5009 / 800-262-1002

> **Restaurant**: Walking distance
>
> **H20**: Outdoor hot tub
>
> **Pet Fee**: $10 per night per pet
>
> **Refundable Pet Deposit**: None
>
> **Size Limit**: None

Terms: Pets cannot be left in room unattended and are not allowed on the furniture. Pets must be registered. Quiet and well-behaved pets only.

Pet Amenities: Dog beds, bowls and treats are provided. Walking distance to National Forest where there are plenty of hiking trails. Professional pet sitting services are also available.

New Summit Inn

1205 North Summit Blvd 80443
970-668-3220 / 800-745-1211

Restaurant: Several within walking distance.

H20: Indoor hot tub

Pet Fee: $10 per night per pet

Refundable Pet Deposit: None

Size Limit: None

Terms: Pets cannot be left in room unattended.

Pet Amenities: Plenty of room to walk pets on property.

Ramada Limited Frisco
990 Lakepoint Drive 80443
970-668-8783 / 888-671-6311

Restaurant: Several within walking distance.

H20: Outdoor hot tub

Pet Fee: $10 per night per pet

Refundable Pet Deposit: None

Size Limit: None

Terms: Well-behaved pet welcome.

Pet Amenities: There are grassy areas on property for walking pets.

Snowshoe Motel
521 Main Street 80443
970-668-3444 / 800-445-8658

Restaurant: Walking distance

H20: Indoor hot tub

Pet Fee: $10 per room per stay

Refundable Pet Deposit: None

Size Limit: None

Terms: Pets cannot be left in room unattended.

Pet Amenities: There are grassy areas nearby to walk pets.

-Glenwood Springs-

Caravan Inn
1826 Grand Avenue 81601
970-945-7451 / 800-945-5495

Restaurant: Several within walking distance.

H20: Seasonal outdoor pool, outdoor hot tub

Pet Fee: $8 per pet per night

Refundable Pet Deposit: None

Size Limit: None

Terms: Pets cannot be left unattended in room.

Pet Amenities: Grassy areas nearby to walk pets.

Hotel Colorado

526 Pine Street 81601

970-945-6511 / 800-544-3998

> **Restaurant**: The Grand Lobby Restaurant, The Palm Court Lounge
>
> **H20**: The hot springs pool is located just across the street.
>
> **Pet Fee**: $10 per day per pet
>
> **Refundable Pet Deposit**: None
>
> **Size Limit**: None
>
> **Terms**: Pets cannot be left unattended in room unless crated.
>
> **Pet Amenities**: Dog treats at check in. Grassy areas around property.
>
> **Fido's Favorite Features**: Ideal location for the hot springs pool, comfortable accommodations. This beautiful and historic hotel is a great weekend getaway.

Hotel Denver

402 7th Street 81601

970-945-6565 / 800-826-8820

> **Restaurant**: Glenwood Canyon Brewing Company
>
> **H20**: None
>
> **Pet Fee**: None
>
> **Refundable Pet Deposit**: None
>
> **Size Limit**: None
>
> **Terms**: Well-behaved pets are welcome.
>
> **Pet Amenities**: There is a great walking trail along the Colorado River, located one block from the hotel.

Quality Inn & Suites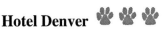

2650 Gilstrap 81601

970-945-5995 / 800-4CHOICE

> **Restaurant**: Several within walking distance.
>
> **H20**: Indoor pool and hot tub
>
> **Pet Fee**: $10 per pet per stay
>
> **Refundable Pet Deposit**: None
>
> **Size Limit**: None
>
> **Terms**: Well-behaved pets only.
>
> **Pet Amenities**: Property located on the river, where there is a walking trail. Grassy areas on property to walk pets.

Ramada Inn
124 West Sixth Street 81601
970-945-2500 / 800-332-1472

> **Restaurant**: 6th Street Bar and Grill
>
> **H20**: Indoor pool and hot tub
>
> **Pet Fee**: $10 per day per pet
>
> **Refundable Pet Deposit**: None
>
> **Size Limit**: None
>
> **Terms**: Well-behaved pets only. Guest is responsible for any damages caused by pets.
>
> **Pet Amenities**: There is nearby park for exercising pets.

-Golden-

Clarion Collection - The Golden Hotel
800 11th Street 80401
303-279-0100 / 800-4CHOICE

> **Restaurant**: Bridgewater Grill
>
> **H20**: None
>
> **Pet Fee**: $10 per stay per pet
>
> **Refundable Pet Deposit**: None
>
> **Size Limit**: Prefer small pets.
>
> **Terms**: Pets cannot be left unattended in room.
>
> **Pet Amenities**: There is a park nearby for exercising pets.

Days Inn Denver West
15059 West Colfax Avenue 80401
303-277-0200 / 800-329-7466

> **Restaurant**: The Daybreak
>
> **H20**: Seasonal outdoor pool, indoor hot tub
>
> **Pet Fee**: $6 per night per room
>
> **Refundable Pet Deposit**: None
>
> **Size Limit**: None
>
> **Terms**: Pets cannot be left unattended in room.
>
> **Pet Amenities**: There is a small grassy area to walk pets.

Denver Marriott West

1717 Denver West Boulevard 80401

303-279-9100 / 800-228-9290

Restaurant: Allie's American Grill, Goldfield's Lounge

H20: Indoor pool and hot tub, seasonal outdoor pool

Pet Fee: $10 per day per pet

Refundable Pet Deposit: None

Size Limit: None

Terms: Well-behaved pets are welcome. Guest is responsible for pet's behavior.

Pet Amenities: Pet rooms are on the first floor and have convenient sliding glass doors which access a grassy area for walking and exercising pets.

Fido's Favorite Features: Great location, comfortable accommodations, plenty of area to walk pets nearby. This convenient location is just off I-70 and is close to the Colorado Mills shopping mall.

Holiday Inn Denver West
14707 W. Colfax Avenue 80401
303-279-7611 / 800-HOLIDAY

> **Restaurant**: The Garden Deck
>
> **H20**: Indoor pool and hot tub
>
> **Pet Fee**: None
>
> **Refundable Pet Deposit**: $20
>
> **Size Limit**: None
>
> **Terms**: Pet rooms have an exterior entrance and are all smoking rooms.
>
> **Pet Amenities**: There are grassy areas around the property to walk your dog.

La Quinta Inn Denver/Golden
3301 Youngfield Service Rd. 80401
303-279-5565 / 800-531-5900

> **Restaurant**: Walking distance
>
> **H20**: Seasonal outdoor pool
>
> **Pet Fee**: None
>
> **Refundable Pet Deposit**: None
>
> **Size Limit**: None
>
> **Terms**: Well-behaved dogs only.
>
> **Pet Amenities**: There is a large field next to the building for walking pets.

Residence Inn Denver West/Golden
14600 W. 6th Avenue 80401
303-271-0909 / 800-331-3131

> **Restaurant**: Short drive
>
> **H20**: Indoor pool and hot tub
>
> **Pet Fee**: $25 per night up to $75 per week
>
> **Refundable Pet Deposit**: None
>
> **Size Limit**: None
>
> **Terms**: Must make arrangements with housekeeping if pet is unattended and not crated.
>
> **Pet Amenities**: There is a large field next to the building to walk your dogs.

Table Mountain Inn

1310 Washington Avenue 80401

303-277-9898 / 800-762-9898

> **Restaurant**: Table Mountain Inn Restaurant
>
> **H20**: None
>
> **Pet Fee**: $10 per night per room
>
> **Refundable Pet Deposit**: None
>
> **Size Limit**: None
>
> **Terms**: Pets cannot be left unattended in room unless crated. Dogs and cats welcome. Guest is responsible for damage caused by pets.
>
> **Pet Amenities**: Pet treats at check in. Front desk will recommend areas for walking pets. Restaurant has steak bones upon request (when available).

-Granby-

The Inn at Silver Creek

62927 U.S. Highway 40 80446

970-887-2131 / 800-926-4386

> **Restaurant**: Creekside Grill
>
> **H20**: Outdoor pool, two outdoor hot tubs, two indoor hot tubs
>
> **Pet Fee**: $25 per pet for 1 or 2 nights stay. $50 per pet for 3 nights or longer.
>
> **Refundable Pet Deposit**: None
>
> **Size Limit**: None
>
> **Terms**: Guest must register pets. Pets cannot be left unattended in room unless crated and are not allowed on furniture. Guest must pick up after pets. Pets must be leashed while in public areas.
>
> **Pet Amenities**: Hiking and snow shoeing trails near hotel. Pet pick up bags and waste receptacles are located at some entrance / exit doors. There are large and small ponds full of ducks and geese for dogs to chase.

"The average dog is nicer than the average person."
-Andrew A. Rooney

-Grand Junction-

Best Western Horizon Inn
754 Horizon Drive 81506
970-245-1410 / 800-544-3782

> **Restaurant**: Walking distance
>
> **H20**: Year round outdoor pool and indoor hot tub
>
> **Pet Fee**: None
>
> **Refundable Pet Deposit**: None
>
> **Size Limit**: None
>
> **Terms**: Must declare pets upon check in. Pets must not be left unattended in room.
>
> **Pet Amenities**: There is plenty of space to walk dogs on property. Dog biscuits at check in.

Best Western Sandman Motel
708 Horizon Drive 81506
970-243-4150 / 800-528-1234

> **Restaurant**: Several within walking distance
>
> **H20**: Seasonal outdoor pool, indoor hot tub
>
> **Pet Fee**: None
>
> **Refundable Pet Deposit**: None
>
> **Size Limit**: None
>
> **Terms**: Pets cannot be left unattended in room.
>
> **Pet Amenities**: There is an area to walk pets nearby.

Budget Host Inn
721 Horizon Drive 81506
970-243-6050 / 800-888-5736

> **Restaurant**: Several within walking distance.
>
> **H20**: Seasonal outdoor pool
>
> **Pet Fee**: None
>
> **Refundable Pet Deposit**: $50
>
> **Size Limit**: None
>
> **Terms**: Pets cannot be left unattended in room.
>
> **Pet Amenities**: There is an area to walk pets on property.

Traveling With Your Pet ...In Style!

Doubletree Hotel Grand Junction
743 Horizon Drive 81506
970-241-8888 / 800-222-TREE

Restaurant: Bistro 743

H20: Seasonal outdoor pool, outdoor hot tub

Pet Fee: $25 per room per stay

Refundable Pet Deposit: None

Size Limit: 40 lbs.

Terms: Well-behaved pets welcome.

Pet Amenities: There are grassy areas galore on property.

Fido's Favorite Features: The pool area, comfortable accommodations, great location off I70. This a fantastic property for pets.

Grand Junction Super 8
728 Horizon Drive 81506
970-248-8080 / 800-800-8000

Restaurant: Several within walking distance.

H20: Seasonal outdoor pool

Pet Fee: $5 per day per pet

Refundable Pet Deposit: None

Size Limit:100 lbs.

Terms: Pets cannot be left unattended in room.

Pet Amenities: There are areas to walk pets nearby.

Grand Vista Hotel
2790 Crossroads Boulevard 81506
970-241-8411 / 800-800-7796

Restaurant: Oliver's, Bailey's Lounge

H20: Indoor pool and hot tub

Pet Fee: $10 per day per pet

Refundable Pet Deposit: None

Size Limit: None

Terms: Well-behaved pets only.

Pet Amenities: Designated pet walk area on property.

Hampton Inn

205 Main Street 81501

970-243-3222 / 877-307-5678

> **Restaurant**: Walking distance
>
> **H20**: Seasonal outdoor pool and hot tub
>
> **Pet Fee**: $25 per day up to $125 per room per stay
>
> **Refundable Pet Deposit**: None
>
> **Size Limit**: 60 lbs.
>
> **Terms**: Well-behaved pets only.
>
> **Pet Amenities**: Pet area located on property.

Hawthorn Suites

225 Main Street 81501

970-242-2525 / 800-922-3883

> **Restaurant**: Walking distance
>
> **H20**: Indoor pool, outdoor hot tub
>
> **Pet Fee**: $25 per day up to $125 per room per stay
>
> **Refundable Pet Deposit**: None
>
> **Size Limit**: 60 lbs.
>
> **Terms**: Well-behaved pets only.
>
> **Pet Amenities**: Pet walking area located on property.
>
> **Fido's Favorite Features**: Convenient downtown location, stylish rooms, friendly staff.

Holiday Inn

755 Horizon Drive 81506

970-243-6790 / 888-489-9796

> **Restaurant**: Coco's Bakery, Restaurant and Bar
>
> **H20**: Indoor pool and hot tub, seasonal outdoor pool and hot tub.
>
> **Pet Fee**: None
>
> **Refundable Pet Deposit**: None
>
> **Size Limit**: None
>
> **Terms**: Prefer that dogs are not left unattended in guest room.
>
> **Pet Amenities**: There is a designated dog walking area in back of the hotel.
>
> **Fido's Favorite Features**: Convenient location off I70, comfortable accommodations, pet-friendly staff.

La Quinta Inn & Suites
2761 Crossroads Boulevard 81506
970-241-2929 / 800-531-5900

Restaurant: Walking distance

H20: Outdoor hot tub, seasonal outdoor pool

Pet Fee: None

Refundable Pet Deposit: None

Size Limit: None

Terms: Well-behaved pets only.

Pet Amenities: There is a pet walking area on property.

Mesa Inn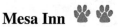
704 Horizon Drive 81506
970-245-3080 / 888-955-3080

Restaurant: Several within walking distance.

H20: Seasonal outdoor pool

Pet Fee: None

Refundable Pet Deposit: $50

Size Limit: None

Terms: Well-behaved pets only.

Pet Amenities: There are grassy areas near property for walking pets.

Quality Inn of Grand Junction
733 Horizon Drive 81506
970-245-7200 / 800-4-CHOICE

Restaurant: Several within walking distance.

H20: Outdoor pool, tented during winter

Pet Fee: None

Refundable Pet Deposit: $50

Size Limit: None

Terms: Well-behaved pets only.

Pet Amenities: Plenty of space behind hotel for walking pets.

Ramada Inn
752 Horizon Drive 81506
970-243-5150 / 800-2RAMADA

> **Restaurant**: Starvin' Arvins
>
> **H20**: Seasonal outdoor pool, outdoor hot tub
>
> **Pet Fee**: $10 per room per stay
>
> **Refundable Pet Deposit**: None
>
> **Size Limit**: None
>
> **Terms**: Well-behaved pets welcome.
>
> **Pet Amenities**: There is a courtyard on property for walking pets.

West Gate Inn
2210 Highway 6 & 50 81505
970-241-3020 / 800-453-9253

> **Restaurant**: Otto's
>
> **H20**: Seasonal outdoor pool
>
> **Pet Fee**: None
>
> **Refundable Pet Deposit**: None
>
> **Size Limit**: None
>
> **Terms**: Well-behaved pets only. Pets cannot be left unattended in room. There are designated pet rooms. Pets must be registered.
>
> **Pet Amenities**: There is a designated pet walking area on property.

-Grand Lake-

Mountain Lakes Lodge
10480 Highway 34 80447
970-627-8448

> **Restaurant**: Short drive
>
> **H20**: None
>
> **Pet Fee**: $10 per day per pet
>
> **Refundable Pet Deposit**: None
>
> **Size Limit**: None
>
> **Terms**: Guest is responsible for damage caused by pets. Pets must be leashed while in public areas.
>
> **Pet Amenities**: River on property for dogs to swim. Biscuits, blankets and towels at check in.

-Greeley-

Best Western Regency Hotel
701 8th Street 80631
970-353-8444 / 800-WESTERN

Restaurant: Lopiano's

H20: Indoor pool

Pet Fee: $25 per pet per stay

Refundable Pet Deposit: None

Size Limit: None

Terms: Pets must be crated if left in room unattended. No grooming or bathing pets in bathtubs. Pets are not allowed on furniture. Four dogs per room is the limit. Please use pet relief areas on property. Guests must clean up after their pets.

Pet Amenities: Pet waste stations are available for your convenience. There is plenty of room to walk your pets on the property.

Country Inn & Suites by Carlson
2501 West 29th Street 80631
970-330-3404 / 800-456-4000

Restaurant: Several within walking distance.

H20: Indoor pool and hot tub

Pet Fee: $15 per night per pet

Refundable Pet Deposit: None

Size Limit: 20 lbs.

Terms: Must be in a smoking room.

Pet Amenities: Plenty of room to walk pets on property.

Make sure your pet is current on all required vaccinations. While on the road, carry proof from your Veterinarian.

Holiday Inn Express
2563 W. 29th Street 80631
970-330-7495 / 800-HOLIDAY

Restaurant: Several within walking distance

H20: Indoor pool and hot tub

Pet Fee: $25 per room per pet.

Refundable Pet Deposit: None

Size Limit: None

Terms: Well-behaved pets only. Guest is responsible for damage caused by pets.

Pet Amenities: There is a pet relief area on property. Pet sitter is available upon request.

Super 8 Motel
2423 West 29th Street 80631
970-330-8880 / 800-800-8000

Restaurant: Walking distance

H20: None

Pet Fee: $20 per night per room

Refundable Pet Deposit: None

Size Limit: None

Terms: Two pet maximum per room.

Pet Amenities: There is a grassy area to walk pets.

-Greenwood Village-

Hampton Inn Denver Southeast
9231 East Arapahoe Road 80112
303-792-9999 / 800-HILTON

Restaurant: Within walking distance

H20: Seasonal outdoor pool

Pet Fee: $10 per night per pet

Refundable Pet Deposit: None

Size Limit: None

Terms: Pets cannot be left unattended in room.

Pet Amenities: There is a grassy area on property to walk pets.

La Quinta Inn & Suites
7077 South Clinton Street 80112
303-649-9969 / 800-531-5900

> **Restaurant**: Walking distance
>
> **H20**: Outdoor hot tub, seasonal outdoor pool
>
> **Pet Fee**: None
>
> **Refundable Pet Deposit**: None
>
> **Size Limit**: 25 lbs.
>
> **Terms**: None
>
> **Pet Amenities**: Dog treats and pet waste bags are available at the front desk. First floor courtyard rooms have a second entrance which accesses the courtyard for walking pets.

Sheraton Hotel Denver Tech Center
7007 S. Clinton Street 80112
303-799-6200 / 800-325-3535

> **Restaurant**: Browsers
>
> **H20**: Outdoor hot tub, seasonal outdoor pool
>
> **Pet Fee**: None
>
> **Refundable Pet Deposit**: None
>
> **Size Limit**: None
>
> **Terms**: Guest must sign a pet agreement claiming responsibility for any damages caused by pet.
>
> **Pet Amenities**: Signature Sheraton pet beds available for use. Ample dog walking space around hotel property. There is plenty of grass and space to exercise pets.
>
> **Fido's Favorite Features**: Very comfortable rooms, convenient location, great happy hour. This is a very nice Sheraton property, well worth checking out.
>
> * You wouldn't want to miss out on Pet Outfitters, it is a nicely stocked, upscale pet store, well worth checking out.

Sleep Inn Denver Tech Center
9257 Costilla Avenue 80112
303-662-9950 / 800-424-6423

> **Restaurant**: Several within walking distance
>
> **H20**: Indoor pool
>
> **Pet Fee**: $25 per room per stay
>
> **Refundable Pet Deposit**: None
>
> **Size Limit**: 40 lbs.
>
> **Terms**: Pets cannot be left in room unattended.
>
> **Pet Amenities**: There is a grassy area on property to walk pets.

Summerfield Suites by Wyndham - Denver
9280 East Costilla Avenue 80112
303-706-1945 / 800-889-8846

> **Restaurant**: Several within walking distance.
>
> **H20**: Seasonal outdoor pool, outdoor hot tub
>
> **Pet Fee**: $150 / One bedroom, $200 / 2 two bedroom, one time fee.
>
> **Refundable Pet Deposit**: None
>
> **Size Limit**: None
>
> **Terms**: Pets cannot be left in room unattended. Owner is responsible to pick up after pets.
>
> **Pet Amenities**: There is a large grassy area on property to walk pets.

Woodfield Suites - Denver Tech Center
9009 E. Arapahoe Rd. 80112
303-799-4555 / 800-338-0008

> **Restaurant**: Walking distance
>
> **H20**: Indoor pool and hot tub
>
> **Pet Fee**: None
>
> **Refundable Pet Deposit**: None
>
> **Size Limit**: None
>
> **Terms**: Unattended pets left in room must be crated. Well-behaved pets only. Pets are not allowed in lobby area.
>
> **Pet Amenities**: Dog or cat welcome bags at check in. There are grassy areas on property for walking pets.

-Gunnison-

Alpine Inn
1011 West Rio Grande 81230
970-641-2804 / 866-299-6648

Restaurant: Short drive

H20: Indoor pool and hot tub

Pet Fee: $10 per stay per pet

Refundable Pet Deposit: None

Size Limit: None

Terms: Pets cannot be left in room unattended.

Pet Amenities: Plenty of grassy areas to walk your pet.

"Knick-knack, paddy whack, give the dog a bone..."
-Unknown

Days Inn
701 Highway 50 81230
970-641-0608 / 888-641-0608

Restaurant: Short drive

H20: Indoor hot tub

Pet Fee: $5 per day per pet

Refundable Pet Deposit: None

Size Limit: None

Terms: Pets should not be left unattended in rooms.

Pet Amenities: Pet walking area next to property.

Water Wheel Inn
37478 West Hwy 50 81230
970-641-1650 / 800-642-1650

Restaurant: Walking distance

H20: Indoor hot tub

Pet Fee: None

Refundable Pet Deposit: None

Size Limit: 75 lbs.

Terms: Pets cannot be left in room unattended. Pets must be leashed at all times while in common areas.

Pet Amenities: Plenty of grass on property to walk pets.

-Highlands Ranch-

Residence Inn Denver South
93 West Centennial Boulevard 80126
303-683-5500 / 800-331-3131

Restaurant: Walking distance

H20: Seasonal outdoor pool and hot tub

Pet Fee: $75 per stay per room

Refundable Pet Deposit: None

Size Limit: None

Terms: Well-behaved pets only. Must make arrangements with housekeeping if pet is unattended in room. Guest is responsible for any damage caused by pets.

Pet Amenities: Grassy area behind hotel to walk pets.

-Hotchkiss-

Hotchkiss Inn
406 Highway 133 81419
970-872-2200 / 800-817-1418
> **Restaurant**: Walking distance
> **H20**: None
> **Pet Fee**: $10 per day per pet
> **Refundable Pet Deposit**: None
> **Size Limit**: None
> **Terms**: Guest is responsible for damages caused by pets.
> **Pet Amenities**: There is a pet walking area on property.

-Hot Sulphur Springs-

Canyon Motel
221 Byers Avenue (Route 40) 80451
970-725-3395 / 888-489-3719
> **Restaurant**: Walking distance
> **H20**: None
> **Pet Fee**: $10 per day per room
> **Refundable Pet Deposit**: None
> **Size Limit**: None
> **Terms**: Must sign pet agreement policy at check in. Pets cannot be left unattended in room. Two dogs per room maximum.
> **Pet Amenities**: Biscuits at check in. Pet sitting available for a fee. There is an open field across the street for walking your dogs.

-Idaho Springs-

H & H Motor Lodge
2445 Colorado Boulevard 80452
303-567-2838 / 800-445-2893
> **Restaurant**: Several restaurants within walking distance.

H20: Indoor hot tub

Pet Fee: $5 per day per pet

Refundable Pet Deposit: None

Size Limit: None

Terms: Guest is responsible for damages caused by pets.

Pet Amenities: There is an open field across the road for walking pets.

-Julesburg-

Budget Host Platte Valley Inn
15225 Highway 385 80737
970-474-3336 / 800-562-5166

Restaurant: The Platte Valley Inn Restaurant

H20: Seasonal outdoor pool

Pet Fee: $7 per dog per day

Refundable Pet Deposit: None

Size Limit: None

Terms: Well-behaved pets only. Must be in smoking rooms. No cats.

Pet Amenities: Pet walking area on property.

-Keystone-

The Inn at Keystone
23044 Hwy 6 80435
970-496-4825 / 877-724-4340

Restaurant: Summit Seafood Restaurant

H20: Three outdoor hot tubs

Pet Fee: $20 per day per pet

Refundable Pet Deposit: None

Size Limit: None

Terms: Pet policy form at check in. Pets must be well-behaved.

Pet Amenities: There are grassy areas nearby to walk your pet.

-La Junta-

Holiday Inn Express
27994 U.S. Highway 50 Frontage Rd. 81050
719-384-2900 / 800-HOLIDAY

Restaurant: Walking distance

H20: Indoor pool and hot tub

Pet Fee: $10 per room per day

Refundable Pet Deposit: None

Size Limit: None

Terms: Pets cannot be left in room unattended. Well-behaved pets only.

Pet Amenities: Pet walking area nearby.

-Lake City-

Crystal Lodge & Restaurant
2175 Highway 149 South 81235
970-944-2201 / 877-GO-LODGE

Restaurant: The Crystal Lodge Restaurant

H20: None

Pet Fee: $25 per stay per room

Refundable Pet Deposit: None

Size Limit: None

Terms: Pets are allowed in suites or cabins only.

Pet Amenities: There is plenty of room for Rover to run.

The ring bearer.

Matterhorn Mountain Motel
409 Bluff Street 81235
970-944-2210

>**Restaurant**: Several restaurants within walking distance.
>
>**H20**: None
>
>**Pet fee**: $10 per stay per pet
>
>**Refundable Pet Deposit**: None
>
>**Size Limit**: None
>
>**Terms**: Pets cannot be left unattended in room. Well-behaved pets welcome.
>
>**Pet Amenities**: Plenty of room to walk your pets.

-Lakewood-

Comfort Suites
11909 West 6th Avenue 80401
303-231-9929 / 800-4CHOICE

>**Restaurant**: Several within walking distance
>
>**H20**: Indoor pool and hot tub
>
>**Pet Fee**: $10 per night per pet
>
>**Refundable Pet Deposit**: None
>
>**Size Limit**: None
>
>**Terms**: Pets cannot be left unattended in room.
>
>**Pet Amenities**: There are grassy areas on property to walk your pets.

La Quinta Inn & Suites Denver
7190 W. Hampden Avenue 80227
303-969-9700 / 800-531-5900

>**Restaurant**: Short drive
>
>**H20**: Outdoor hot tub, seasonal outdoor pool
>
>**Pet Fee**: None
>
>**Refundable Pet Deposit**: None
>
>**Size Limit**: None
>
>**Terms**: None
>
>**Pet Amenities**: There is a pet walking area located on property.

Quality Suites Lakewood

7260 West Jefferson Avenue 80235
303-988-8600 / 800-4CHOICE

> **Restaurant**: Several within walking distance.
>
> **H20**: Indoor pool and two hot tubs
>
> **Pet Fee**: $10 per night per pet
>
> **Refundable Pet Deposit**: None
>
> **Size Limit**: None
>
> **Terms**: Well-behaved pets only.
>
> **Pet Amenities**: There is a field next to the property for walking pets.

Residence Inn Denver Southwest

7050 W. Hampden Avenue 80227
303-985-7676 / 800-331-3131

> **Restaurant**: Several within walking distance.
>
> **H20**: Indoor pool and hot tub
>
> **Pet Fee**: $75 one time fee per stay per room
>
> **Refundable Pet Deposit**: None
>
> **Size Limit**: None
>
> **Terms**: Number of pets is based on the hotel's discretion. Call ahead for best results.
>
> **Pet Amenities**: Dog treats upon check in. Pet walking services can be arranged through the front desk.

Sheraton - Denver West Hotel

360 Union Blvd. 80228
303-987-2000 / 800-325-3535

> **Restaurant**: The Red Rocks Grille
>
> **H20**: Indoor pool and hot tub
>
> **Pet Fee**: None
>
> **Refundable Pet Deposit**: None
>
> **Size Limit**: 80 lbs.
>
> **Terms**: Pets cannot be left in room unattended.
>
> **Pet Amenities**: Signature Sheraton pet beds for use. Ample space to walk pets on property.
>
> **Fido's Favorite Features**: The open space for walking pets, convenient location, pet-friendly staff.

TownePlace Suites by Marriott
800 Tabor Street 80215
303-232-7790 / 800-257-3000

    Restaurant: Walking distance

    H20: Seasonal outdoor pool

    Pet Fee: $20 per day per room / $200 maximum per stay

    Refundable Pet Deposit: None

    Size Limit: None

    Terms: No Rottweilers or Pitt Bulls. Pet must be crated if left in room unattended or arrangements must be made for housekeeping to service room.

    Pet Amenities: Pet walking area located on property.

-Lamar-

Best Western Cow Palace Inn
1301 N. Main Street 81052
719-336-7753 / 800-678-0344

    Restaurant: Oasis Restaurant

    H20: Indoor pool and hot tub

    Pet Fee: None

    Refundable Pet Deposit: None

    Size Limit: None

    Terms: Guest is responsible for damage caused by pets.

    Pet Amenities: There is an ample pet walking area behind the building.

Blue Spruce Motel
1801 South Main Street 81052
719-336-7454

    Restaurant: Within walking distance

    H20: Seasonal outdoor pool

    Pet Fee: $5 per day per pet

    Refundable Pet Deposit: None

    Size Limit: None

    Terms: Pets cannot be left unattended in room.

    Pet Amenities: There is an area on property to walk pets.

El Mar Budget Host Motel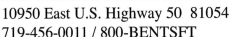
1210 South Main Street 81052
719-336-4331

Restaurant: Within walking distance

H20: Seasonal outdoor pool

Pet Fee: $5 per day per pet

Refundable Pet Deposit: $20

Size Limit: None

Terms: Pets must be in smoking room.

Pet Amenities: There is an area on property to walk pets.

-Las Animas-

Best Western Bent's Fort Inn
10950 East U.S. Highway 50 81054
719-456-0011 / 800-BENTSFT

Restaurant: The Bent's Fort Inn

H20: Seasonal outdoor pool

Pet Fee: None

Refundable Pet Deposit: None

Size Limit: None

Terms: Well-behaved pets welcome.

Pet Amenities: A pet walking area is located on property.

-Leadville-

Alps Motel
S. Hwy 24 80461
719-486-1223 / 800-818-2577

Restaurant: Several within walking distance

H20: None

Pet Fee: $10 per day for one pet, $15 per day for two pets.

Refundable Pet Deposit: None

Size Limit: None

Terms: Pet policy at check in. Owner is responsible for pet's behavior.

Pet Amenities: Nearby areas to walk pets.

-Limon-

Best Western Limon Inn
925 T Avenue 80828
719-775-0277 / 800-528-1234

> **Restaurant**: Walking distance
>
> **H20**: Indoor pool and hot tub
>
> **Pet Fee**: $10 per stay per room
>
> **Refundable Pet Deposit**: None
>
> **Size Limit**: None
>
> **Terms**: There are only four designated pet rooms, best to call in advance.
>
> **Pet Amenities**: Designated pet walking area on property.

Super 8 Motel
937 Highway 24 80828
719-775-2889 / 800-800-8000

> **Restaurant**: Within walking distance
>
> **H20**: None
>
> **Pet Fee**: $10 per room per stay
>
> **Refundable Pet Deposit**: None
>
> **Size Limit**: None
>
> **Terms**: Pets cannot be left unattended in room.
>
> **Pet Amenities**: There is a grassy area to walk pets on property.

Tyme Square Inn
2505 6th Street 80828
719-775-0700 / 877-900-TYME

> **Restaurant**: Walking distance
>
> **H20**: Indoor pool and hot tub
>
> **Pet Fee**: $15 per day per pet
>
> **Refundable Pet Deposit**: None
>
> **Size Limit**: None
>
> **Terms**: Pets cannot be left unattended in rooms. Guest is responsible for damages caused by pets. Guest must pick up after pets.
>
> **Pet Amenities**: Pet walking area is located near the property.

-Littleton-

Amerisuites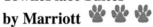
9030 East Westview Road 80124
303-662-8500 / 800-833-1516

Restaurant: Walking distance

H20: Indoor pool

Pet Fee: $10 per day per pet

Refundable Pet Deposit: None

Size Limit: 50 lbs.

Terms: Well-behaved pets welcome.

Pet Amenities: There are grassy areas on the property to walk pets.

TownePlace Suites
by Marriott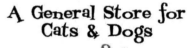
10920 W. Toller Drive 80127
303-972-0555 / 800-257-3000

Restaurant: Short drive

H20: Seasonal outdoor pool

Pet Fee: $75 one time fee per stay

Refundable Pet Deposit: None

Size Limit: None

Terms: Pets must be house trained and well-behaved.

Pet Amenities: Treats at check in, pet walking area on property. Flexible housekeeping to accommodate guest's schedule with pets.

* While in Littleton, Lewis and Bark is a must. They carry a full line of natural goodies and other wonderful products for your pooch.

STAYBRIDGE SUITES

DENVER SOUTH - LONE TREE
7820 PARK MEADOWS DRIVE LONE TREE, CO 80124

Staybridge Suites Welcomes You... And Our Pet Guests!

We recognize that having your pet family members with you adds an additional level of comfort while your are away from home.

All pets must be housebroken.
No more than two pets per suite.
All cats must be declawed.

We look forward to seeing you.
We reserve the right to refuse certain pets.

For reservations or details, please call 303-649-1010.
Or visit our website at www.staybridge.com.

-Lone Tree-

Staybridge Suites
7820 Park Meadows Drive 80124
303-649-1010 / 800-238-8000

Restaurant: Walking distance

H20: Seasonal outdoor pool

Pet Fee: $20 per night per room for the first four nights or $100 flat fee for the entire length of stay.

Refundable Pet Deposit: None

Size Limit: None

Terms: Well-behaved pets welcome. Cats must be declawed. Two pets per suite maximum.

Pet Amenities: Generous dog walking area on South side of hotel.

Fido's Favorite Features: The included expanded breakfast, comfortable and spacious suites, very friendly staff. This location is less than two miles to Park Meadows shopping mall.

-Longmont-

Hawthorn Suites
2000 Sunset Way 80501
303-774-7100 / 800-527-1133

Restaurant: Several within walking distance.

H20: Seasonal outdoor pool and hot tub

Pet Fee: None

Refundable Pet Deposit: $50

Size Limit: None

Terms: Pets cannot be left unattended in room.

Pet Amenities: There are grassy areas to walk pets nearby.

"I named my dog Stay... so I can say
'Come here, Stay. Come here, Stay'."
-Steven Wright

Radisson Hotel & Conference Center
1900 Ken Pratt Boulevard 80501
303-776-2000 / 800-333-3333

> **Restaurant**: The Whetstone Steakhouse, Heritage Club Lounge
>
> **H20**: Seasonal outdoor pool
>
> **Pet Fee**: None
>
> **Refundable Pet Deposit**: $50
>
> **Size Limit**: None
>
> **Terms**: Pets cannot be left unattended in room.
>
> **Pet Amenities**: There are areas to walk pets on property.

Residence Inn
1450 Dry Creek Drive 80503
303-702-9933 / 800-331-3131

> **Restaurant**: Walking distance
>
> **H20**: Indoor pool and hot tub
>
> **Pet Fee**: $50 for one to six nights, $100 for seven or more nights.
>
> **Refundable Pet Deposit**: None
>
> **Size Limit**: 75 lbs.
>
> **Terms**: Two pets per room maximum.
>
> **Pet Amenities**: Pet welcome bag, dog walk on property, there is a pet store half a mile away.

Travelodge
3815 Highway 119 80504
303-776-8700 / 800-578-7878

> **Restaurant**: Simon's Bar & Grill
>
> **H20**: None
>
> **Pet Fee**: $10 per day per pet/ $50 per week maximum
>
> **Refundable Pet Deposit**: $50
>
> **Size Limit**: None
>
> **Terms**: Well-behaved pets only. Deposit is returned after housekeeping inspection.
>
> **Pet Amenities**: Plenty of grassy areas on property for walking pet.

-Louisville-

Comfort Inn of Boulder County
1196 Dillon Road 80027
303-604-0181 / 800-228-5150

> **Restaurant**: Walking distance
>
> **H20**: None
>
> **Pet Fee**: None
>
> **Refundable Pet Deposit**: $100
>
> **Size Limit**: None
>
> **Terms**: Must be in a smoking room. Guest is responsible for damages caused by pets.
>
> **Pet Amenities**: There is a pet walk area on property.

La Quinta Inn & Suites
902 Dillon Rd. 80027
303-664-0100 / 800-531-5900

> **Restaurant**: Walking distance
>
> **H20**: Outdoor hot tub, seasonal outdoor pool
>
> **Pet Fee**: None
>
> **Refundable Pet Deposit**: None
>
> **Size Limit**: 25 lbs.
>
> **Terms**: Must sign pet agreement at check in. Pets cannot be left in room unattended.
>
> **Pet Amenities**: There is a nice pet walking area behind the hotel.

Residence Inn Boulder/Louisville
845 Coal Creek Circle 80027
303-665-2661 / 800-228-9290

> **Restaurant**: Several within walking distance
>
> **H20**: Indoor pool and hot tub
>
> **Pet Fee**: $75 one time fee per stay
>
> **Refundable Pet Deposit**: None
>
> **Size Limit**: None
>
> **Terms**: Must declare pets at check in.
>
> **Pet Amenities**: Walking trails located near hotel. Plenty of areas to walk pets on property.

-Loveland-

Best Western Coach House
5542 East U.S. Highway 34 80537
970-667-7810 / 888-818-6223

> **Restaurant**: The Blue Note
>
> **H20**: Indoor pool and two hot tubs
>
> **Pet Fee**: $15 one time fee per room
>
> **Refundable Pet Deposit**: None
>
> **Size Limit**: None
>
> **Terms**: Well-behaved pets welcome
>
> **Pet Amenities**: There is plenty of space to walk your dog on property.
>
> *Be sure to drop by Rocky Mountain Pet Outfitters while visiting Loveland. They offer an enormous selection of high quality foods, treats, products and supplies.

Two Eagles Resort
1372 Big Thompson Canyon 80537
970-663-5532 / 866-834-4744

> **Restaurant**: Lengthy drive
>
> **H20**: Outdoor hot tub
>
> **Pet Fee**: $10 per night per pet
>
> **Refundable Pet Deposit**: $250
>
> **Size Limit**: None
>
> **Terms**: Pets cannot be left alone in room. Pets must be leashed while in common areas. Must pick up after pets.
>
> **Pet Amenities**: Treats at check in, pet towels and clean up bags provided. There is a designated pet walk area on property.

-Manitou Springs-

Silver Saddle Motel
215 Manitou Avenue 80829
719-685-5611 / 800-772-3353

> **Restaurant**: Walking distance
>
> **H20**: Seasonal outdoor pool and hot tub
>
> **Pet Fee**: None
>
> **Refundable Pet Deposit**: None
>
> **Size Limit**: None
>
> **Terms**: Well-behaved pets only.
>
> **Pet Amenities**: There are areas to walk pets nearby.

Baylei Bellamy

Baylei and her mom Molly

-Marble-

Ute Meadows Inn B & B and Nordic Center
2280 County Rd. 3 81623
970-963-7088 / 888-883-6323

Restaurant: Walking distance to lunch deli. Otherwise lengthy drive.

H20: Outdoor hot tub

Pet Fee: $15 per night per pet

Refundable Pet Deposit: None

Size Limit: None

Terms: Pets cannot be left unattended in rooms. No cats allowed.

Pet Amenities: Kennels provided, biscuits at check in, pets are allowed on nordic trails.

-Monarch-

Monarch Mountain Lodge & Restaurant
22720 West U.S. Highway 50 81227
719-539-2581 / 800-332-3668

Restaurant: Cliffhangers

H20: Indoor pool, two outdoor hot tubs

Pet Fee: $15 per night per pet

Refundable Pet Deposit: None

Size Limit: None

Terms: Guests are responsible for damage caused by pets.

Pet Amenities: There are ample walking areas and hiking trails near the lodge.

-Monte Vista-

Best Western Movie Manor Motel
2830 West U.S. 160 81144
719-852-5921 / 800-771-9468

Restaurant: Walking distance

H20: None

Pet Fee: $5 per day per pet

Refundable Pet Deposit: None

Size Limit: 30 lbs.

Terms: Must be in a smoking room.

Pet Amenities: There is a designated pet walking area on property.

-Montrose-

Affordable Inns
1480 South Townsend 81401
970-249-6644 / 888-681-4159

Restaurant: Several within walking distance.

H20: Indoor pool and hot tub

Pet Fee: $6 per day per pet

Refundable Pet Deposit: None

Size Limit: None

Terms: No puppies or cats. Pets cannot be left unattended in room.

Pet Amenities: Designated pet walk area.

Best Western Red Arrow Inn
1702 E. Main Street 81402
970-249-9641 / 800-468-9323

Restaurant: Walking distance

H20: Indoor hot tub, seasonal outdoor pool

Pet Fee: $8 per day per pet

Refundable Pet Deposit: None

Size Limit: None

Terms: Well-behaved pets welcome. Barkers cannot be left alone in room.

Pet Amenities: Doggie welcome bag at check in. Huge grassy area to exercise pets.

"If you can't decide between a Shepherd,
a Setter, or a Poodle, get them all... adopt a mutt."
-ASPCA

Black Canyon Motel
1605 E. Main Street 81401
970-249-3495 / 800-348-3495

> **Restaurant**: Walking distance
> **H20**: Seasonal outdoor pool and hot tub
> **Pet Fee**: $5 per stay per pet
> **Refundable Pet Deposit**: None
> **Size Limit**: None
> **Terms**: Well-behaved pets welcome.
> **Pet Amenities**: Designated pet walk area on property.

Canyon Trails Inn
1225 East Main Street 81401
970-249-3426 / 800-858-5991

> **Restaurant**: Within walking distance
> **H20**: Seasonal outdoor hot tub
> **Pet Fee**: None
> **Refundable Pet Deposit**: $10
> **Size Limit**: None
> **Terms**: Pets cannot be left unattended in room.
> **Pet Amenities**: There are grassy areas nearby for walking pets.

Holiday Inn Express Hotel & Suites
1391 S. Townsend Avenue 81401
970-240-1800 / 800-550-9252

> **Restaurant**: Walking distance
> **H20**: Indoor pool and hot tub, outdoor hot tub
> **Pet Fee**: None
> **Refundable Pet Deposit**: None
> **Size Limit**: None
> **Terms**: Designated first floor rooms only, all non-smoking. Pets cannot be left unattended in room.
> **Pet Amenities**: There are ample walking areas around property to walk pets.

Quality Inn & Suites
2751 Commercial Way 81401
970-249-1011 / 800-228-5150

Restaurant: Walking distance

H20: Indoor pool and hot tub

Pet Fee: $5 per day for small dogs, $10 per day for large dogs

Refundable Pet Deposit: None

Size Limit: None

Terms: Pets cannot be left unattended in room.

Pet Amenities: There is a large field next to the property for walking pets.

Western Motel
1200 East Main Street 81401
970-249-3481 / 800-445-7301

Restaurant: Several within walking distance.

H20: Seasonal outdoor pool and hot tub

Pet Fee: $5 per room per stay

Refundable Pet Deposit: None

Size Limit: None

Terms: Well-behaved pets welcome.

Pet Amenities: There are grassy areas to walk pets nearby.

-Nederland-

Best Western Lodge at Nederland
55 Lakeview Drive 80466
303-258-9463 / 800-279-9463

Restaurant: Several within walking distance

H20: Indoor hot tub

Pet Fee: $10 per day per pet

Refundable Pet Deposit: None

Size Limit: None

Terms: Must make arrangements with housekeeping to have room serviced if pet is left unattended. Well-behaved pets only.

Pet Amenities: There is plenty of room to walk your dog on property.

-New Castle-

New Castle Rodeway Inn
781 Burning Mountain Road 81647
970-984-2363 / 800-4CHOICE

Restaurant: Within walking distance.

H20: Indoor pool and hot tub

Pet Fee: $10 per stay per room.

Refundable Pet Deposit: None

Size Limit: None

Terms: Pets cannot be left unattended in room.

Pet Amenities: There is a grassy area in the parking lot to walk pets.

-Northglenn-

Ramada Plaza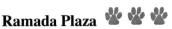
10 East 120th Avenue 80233
303-452-4100 / 800-2RAMADA

Restaurant: Damon's Bar & Grill

H20: Indoor pool and hot tub

Pet Fee: None

Refundable Pet Deposit: $15

Size Limit: None

Terms: Pets cannot be left unattended in room.

Pet Amenities: There is a large park and nice walking path behind the hotel.

-Ouray-

Comfort Inn
191 5th Avenue 81427
970-325-7203 / 800-4385713

Restaurant: Several within walking distance.

H20: Outdoor hot tub

Pet Fee: $10 per night per pet

Refundable Pet Deposit: None

Size Limit: None

Terms: Well-behaved pets only. Pets cannot be left in room unattended.

Pet Amenities: There is plenty of room to walk your pets in the area.

Ouray Victorian Inn
50 Third Avenue 81427
970-325-7222 / 800-443-7361

Restaurant: Walking distance

H20: Two outdoor hot tubs

Pet Fee: None

Refundable Pet Deposit: None

Size Limit: None

Terms: Pets are not allowed in rooms without the owner present.

Pet Amenities: Pet relief area on property, hiking trails nearby.

-Pagosa Springs-

Best Western Oak Ridge Lodge
158 Hot Springs Boulevard 81147
970-264-4173 / 866-472-4672

Restaurant: Squirrel's Pub & Pantry

H20: Indoor pool, outdoor hot tub

Pet Fee: $15 per stay per pet

Refundable Pet Deposit: $100

Size Limit: None

Terms: Well-behaved pets welcome. Pets cannot be left in room unattended.

Pet Amenities: Dog treats available if notified in advance about pet. Hiking trails, a river and walking paths are all within one block.

"The more people I meet, the more I like my dog."
-Anonymous

Fireside Inn Cabins 🐾 🐾
1600 East Hwy 160 81147
970-264-9204 / 888-264-9204

> **Restaurant**: Short drive
>
> **H20**: Outdoor hot tub
>
> **Pet Fee**: $5 per day per pet
>
> **Refundable Pet Deposit**: None
>
> **Size Limit**: None
>
> **Terms**: Two dog maximum per cabin. Call for more info on pet policy.
>
> **Pet Amenities**: Plenty of room to walk pets on property. The cabins are located near the San Juan River.

The Pagosa Springs Inn & Suites 🐾 🐾
519 Village Drive 81147
970-731-3400 / 888-221-8088

> **Restaurant**: Several within walking distance.
>
> **H20**: Indoor pool and hot tub
>
> **Pet Fee**: $10 per night per pet
>
> **Refundable Pet Deposit**: None
>
> **Size Limit**: None
>
> **Terms**: Well-behaved pets welcome.
>
> **Pet Amenities**: There is ample space to walk pets on property.

Pagosa High Country Best Value Lodge

3821 Highway 160 East 81147

970-264-4181 / 800-862-3707

Restaurant: Short drive

H20: Two outdoor covered hot tubs

Pet Fee: $15 per stay per pet

Refundable Pet Deposit: None

Size Limit: None

Terms: Must sign pet policy agreement form at check in. Guest is responsible for any damages.

Pet Amenities: Water and food dishes, pet waste bags and treats at check in. Fifteen wooded acres behind hotel to hike with your dog.

"I wonder if other dogs think poodles are part of a weird religious cult."

-Rita Rudner

The Springs Resort
465 Hot Springs Blvd. 81147
970-264-4168 / 800-225-0934

 Restaurant: Several within walking distance.

 H20: Seventeen hot springs pools

 Pet Fee: $20 per night per pet

 Refundable Pet Deposit: None

 Size Limit: None

 Terms: Must sign pet policy agreement form at check in. Pets cannot be left unattended in room.

 Pet Amenities: Ample space to walk pets on and near property. Property is located on the San Juan River. Local hotel pet tag given at check in.

Super 8 Motel
8 Soloman Drive 81147
970-731-4005 / 800-800-8000

 Restaurant: Short drive

 H20: Indoor hot tub

 Pet Fee: None

 Refundable Pet Deposit: None

 Size Limit: None

 Terms: Pets cannot be left unattended in room.

 Pet Amenities: There is plenty of space to walk your dog on and near the property.

-Pueblo-

Best Western Town House Motel
730 North Santa Fe Avenue 81003
719-543-6530 / 800-WESTERN

 Restaurant: Momo Japanese Restaurant

 H20: Seasonal outdoor pool

 Pet Fee: $10 per room per stay

 Refundable Pet Deposit: None

 Size Limit: None

 Terms: Well-behaved pets welcome.

 Pet Amenities: There is ample space to walk pets on property.

Hampton Inn
4703 North Freeway 81008
719-544-4700 / 800-972-0165

> **Restaurant**: Several within walking distance.
>
> **H20**: Seasonal outdoor pool
>
> **Pet Fee**: $25 per stay per pet
>
> **Refundable Pet Deposit**: None
>
> **Size Limit**: None
>
> **Terms**: Pets cannot be left unattended in room.
>
> **Pet Amenities**: There are grassy areas on property for walking pets.

Holiday Inn Pueblo
4001 N. Elizabeth Street 81108
719-543-8050 / 800-HOLIDAY

> **Restaurant**: Traditions
>
> **H20**: Indoor pool and hot tub
>
> **Pet Fee**: $10 per room per stay
>
> **Refundable Pet Deposit**: None
>
> **Size Limit**: None
>
> **Terms**: Barkers cannot be left unattended in room. They ask that you use good judgment and are respectful of other guests in the hotel.
>
> **Pet Amenities**: Welcome bag at check in containing treats and pet pick up bag. There is a designated dog walk in back of hotel.

La Quinta Inn & Suites Pueblo
4801 North Elizabeth Street 81008
719-542-3500 / 800-531-5900

> **Restaurant**: Several within walking distance.
>
> **H20**: Seasonal outdoor pool, outdoor hot tub
>
> **Pet Fee**: None
>
> **Refundable Pet Deposit**: None
>
> **Size Limit**: 20 lbs.
>
> **Terms**: Must sign a pet policy agreement upon check in.
>
> **Pet Amenities**: There are grassy areas on property for walking pets.

Microtel Inn & Suites
3343 Gateway Drive 81004
719-242-2020 / 888-771-7171

>**Restaurant**: Several within walking distance.
>
>**H20**: None
>
>**Pet Fee**: $10 per room per stay
>
>**Refundable Pet Deposit**: $50
>
>**Size Limit**: None
>
>**Terms**: Well-behaved pets only.
>
>**Pet Amenities**: Plenty of grass on property for walking pets. Large open field next to hotel.

Sleep Inn
3626 North Freeway 81108
719-583-4000 / 800-4CHOICE

>**Restaurant**: Several within walking distance.
>
>**H20**: Indoor pool and hot tub
>
>**Pet Fee**: $15 per stay per pet
>
>**Refundable Pet Deposit**: None
>
>**Size Limit**: None
>
>**Terms**: Pets cannot be left unattended in room.
>
>**Pet Amenities**: Grassy areas to walk pets on property.

-Pueblo West-

Inn at Pueblo West
201 South McCulloch Blvd. 81007
719-547-2111 / 800-448-1972

>**Restaurant**: Tuscany Vineyards
>
>**H20**: Seasonal outdoor pool
>
>**Pet Fee**: None
>
>**Refundable Pet Deposit**: $50
>
>**Size Limit**: None
>
>**Terms**: Must sign pet policy agreement form at check in.
>
>**Pet Amenities**: Plenty of grassy areas for walking pets on property.

-Redstone-

Avalanche Ranch
12863 Highway 133 81623
970-963-2846 / 877-963-9339

> **Restaurant**: Short drive
>
> **H20**: Outdoor hot tub
>
> **Pet Fee**: $12 per night per pet, two pets per cabin maximum.
>
> **Refundable Pet Deposit**: None
>
> **Size Limit**: None
>
> **Terms**: Pets cannot be left unattended in cars or cabins for long periods of time.
>
> **Pet Amenities**: Welcome treats, pet towels and pet waste bags available. Dog beds on request. Large property to run dogs. There is also a river and a pond forpets to enjoy. Kennels and pet services nearby.

Redstone Inn
82 Redstone Boulevard 81623
970-963-2526 / 800-748-2524

> **Restaurant**: The Dining Room, The Bar & Grill
>
> **H20**: Year round outdoor pool and hot tub
>
> **Pet Fee**: $15 per stay per pet
>
> **Refundable Pet Deposit**: None
>
> **Size Limit**: None
>
> **Terms**: There are four pet rooms available; each is ground level with two queen beds. Two pets per room maximum. Guests must pick up after their pets.
>
> **Pet Amenities**: There are several walking trails nearby and the river for dogs to swim. There is plenty of grass on property for walking pets.
>
> **Fido's Favorite Features**: The pool area, lots of grass for Fido, good restaurants. This impressive historic property offers a unique and unforgettable experience.

River's Edge
15184 Highway 133 81623
970-963-8368

> **Restaurant**: Short drive
>
> **H20**: None
>
> **Pet Fee**: No charge for first two pets. Additional pets are $15 per night per pet.
>
> **Refundable Pet Deposit**: None
>
> **Size Limit**: None
>
> **Terms**: Well-behaved pets welcome.
>
> **Pet Amenities**: Jar of biscuits, pet towels, plenty of room for dogs to run. There is a private entrance with a riverside deck. There is a fenced in yard for pets to run and play.

-Ridgway-

Ridgway/Ouray Lodge & Suites
373 Palomino Trail 81432
970-626-5444 / 800-368-5444

> **Restaurant**: Walking distance
>
> **H20**: Indoor pool and hot tub
>
> **Pet Fee**: $10 per night per pet
>
> **Refundable Pet Deposit**: None
>
> **Size Limit**: None
>
> **Terms**: Pets cannot be left unattended in room.
>
> **Pet Amenities**: There is plenty of open space to exercise your pets.

Chipeta Sun Lodge & Spa
304 South Lena Street 81432
970-626-3737 / 800-633-5868

> **Restaurant**: Several within walking distance.
>
> **H20**: Seasonal outdoor pool and hot tub, indoor hot tub
>
> **Pet Fee**: $35 per stay per room.
>
> **Refundable Pet Deposit**: None
>
> **Size Limit**: Prefer smaller pets.
>
> **Terms**: Well-behaved pets only.
>
> **Pet Amenities**: There is ample space to walk pets nearby.

-Rifle-

Red River Inn

718 Taughenbaugh Boulevard 81650
970-625-3050 / 800-733-3152

> **Restaurant**: Walking distance
>
> **H20**: None
>
> **Pet Fee**: $10 per day per pet
>
> **Refundable Pet Deposit**: None
>
> **Size Limit**: None
>
> **Terms**: Pets cannot be left unattended in room. Must be in smoking rooms.
>
> **Pet Amenities**: There are areas to walk your pets on property.

Rusty Canyon Motel

701 Taughenbaugh Boulevard 81650
970-625-4004 / 866-625-4004

> **Restaurant**: Walking distance
>
> **H20**: Outdoor pool (tented in winter)
>
> **Pet Fee**: $25 per stay per pet
>
> **Refundable Pet Deposit**: $25
>
> **Size Limit**: None
>
> **Terms**: Pets cannot be left unattended in room. Guest is responsible for any damages caused by pets.
>
> **Pet Amenities**: There is plenty of room to walk your dog on property.

Loungin'

-Salida-

Best Western Colorado Lodge
352 West Rainbow Blvd. 81201
719-539-2514 / 800-777-7947
> **Restaurant**: Several within walking distance.
>
> **H20**: Indoor pool and hot tub
>
> **Pet Fee**: $10 per night per pet
>
> **Refundable Pet Deposit**: None
>
> **Size Limit**: None
>
> **Terms**: Pets cannot be left unattended in room.
>
> **Pet Amenities**: There are areas to walk your pets nearby.

Days Inn
407 East Hwy 50 81201
719-539-6651 / 800-DAYSINN
> **Restaurant**: Walking distance
>
> **H20**: Outdoor hot tub
>
> **Pet Fee**: $10 per night per pet
>
> **Refundable Pet Deposit**: None
>
> **Size Limit**: None
>
> **Terms**: Pets cannot be left unattended in room.
>
> **Pet Amenities**: There are grassy areas on property to walk pets.

Econo Lodge
1310 East Hwy 50 81201
719-539-2895 / 800-553-2666
> **Restaurant**: Several within walking distance.
>
> **H20**: Outdoor covered hot tub
>
> **Pet Fee**: $10 per night per room
>
> **Refundable Pet Deposit**: None
>
> **Size Limit**: 40 lbs.
>
> **Terms**: One pet per room maximum.
>
> **Pet Amenities**: There is a grassy area on property for walking pets.

Super 8 Motel
525 West Rainbow Blvd. 81201
719-539-6689 / 800-800-8000

Restaurant: Several within walking distance.

H20: Indoor pool and hot tub

Pet Fee: None

Refundable Pet Deposit: None

Size Limit: None

Terms: Must declare pets at check in.

Pet Amenities: There are plenty of areas nearby for walking pets.

Travelodge
7310 Highway 50 81201
719-539-2528 / 800-234-1077

Restaurant: Walking distance to several

H20: Two outdoor hot tubs, seasonal outdoor pool

Pet Fee: $5 per night per pet

Refundable Pet Deposit: None

Size Limit: None

Terms: Well-behaved pets welcome. Damages charged to credit card.

Pet Amenities: Pet welcome bag at check in. There is plenty of room to walk pets on property. Pet-friendly staff.

-Silverthorne-

Days Inn Summit County
580 Silverthorne Lane 80498
970-468-8661 / 800-800-8000

Restaurant: Several within walking distance

H20: Indoor pool and hot tub

Pet Fee: $10 per night per pet

Refundable Pet Deposit: None

Size Limit: None

Terms: Pets cannot be left unattended in room.

Pet Amenities: There are grassy areas on property for walking pets

La Quinta Inn & Suites
560 Silverthorne Lane 80498
970-468-6200 / 800-321-3509
> **Restaurant**: Old Chicago
> **H20**: Indoor pool and hot tub
> **Pet Fee**: $20 per stay per pet
> **Refundable Pet Deposit**: None
> **Size Limit**: 35 lbs.
> **Terms**: Pets cannot be left unattended in room.
> **Pet Amenities**: There is ample space on property for walking pets.

Quality Inn & Suites Summit County
530 Silverthorne Lane 80498
970-513-1222 / 800-4CHOICE
> **Restaurant**: Walking distance
> **H20**: Indoor pool and hot tub, outdoor hot tub
> **Pet Fee**: $10 per night per pet
> **Refundable Pet Deposit**: None
> **Size Limit**: None
> **Terms**: There is a limited amount of pet rooms, best to call in advance.
> **Pet Amenities**: There are ample walking areas on property and nearby. Pet pick up bags are available at the front desk.

-Silverton-

The Wyman Hotel & Inn
1371 Greene Street 81433
970-387-5372 / 800-609-7845
> **Restaurant**: The Dining Room
> **H20**: None
> **Pet Fee**: $25 per stay per pet
> **Refundable Pet Deposit**: None
> **Size Limit**: None
> **Terms**: Pets cannot be left unattended in room if they bark. Well-behaved, house trained pets are welcome.
> **Pet Amenities**: Dog biscuits at the time of afternoon tea. Pet sitter / walker available upon request for an additional fee.

-South Fork-

Comfort Inn at South Fork
182 East Frontage Road 81154
719-873-5600 / 800-228-5150

Restaurant: Walking distance

H20: Indoor pool and hot tub

Pet Fee: $10 per night per pet

Refundable Pet Deposit: None

Size Limit: 60 lbs.

Terms: Pets cannot be left in room unattended. There are designated pet rooms.

Pet Amenities: There is plenty of room to exercise pets on property.

Wolf Creek Lodge
31042 West Highway 160 81154
719-873-5547 / 800-874-0416

Restaurant: Walking distance

H20: Three outdoor hot tubs

Pet Fee: $10 per night per pet

Refundable Pet Deposit: None

Size Limit: None

Terms: Must register pets, those who don't declare pets at check-in will have a pet fee added to their final bill. Pets must be leashed while in common areas. Two pet maximum per room. No cats allowed.

Pet Amenities: There is plenty of room to walk pets behind the lodge.

"Outside of a dog, a book is a man's best friend... and inside a dog, it's too dark to read."

-Groucho Marx

-Steamboat Springs-

The Alpiner Lodge
424 Lincoln Avenue 80477
970-879-1430 / 800-340-9169

> **Restaurant**: Within walking distance to several.
>
> **H20**: None
>
> **Pet Fee**: $10 per stay per room
>
> **Refundable Pet Deposit**: None
>
> **Size Limit**: None
>
> **Terms**: One dog per room maximum. Pets cannot be left unattended for long periods of time. No barkers, please.
>
> **Pet Amenities**: There are areas nearby for walking pets.

Comfort Inn

1055 Walton Creek Road 80487
970-879-6669 / 800-937-5869

> **Restaurant**: Within walking distance
> **H20**: Indoor pool and hot tub
> **Pet Fee**: $10 per night per pet
> **Refundable Pet Deposit**: $100
> **Size Limit**: None
> **Terms**: Pets cannot be left unattended in room.
> **Pet Amenities**: There is ample space on property for walking pets.

"A little dog will do you good."

-Anonymous

Fairfield Inn & Suites by Marriott

3200 South Lincoln Avenue 80487
970-870-9000 / 800-228-2800

> **Restaurant**: Walking distance
>
> **H20**: Indoor pool and hot tub
>
> **Pet Fee**: $50 per stay per pet
>
> **Refundable Pet Deposit**: $100
>
> **Size Limit**: None
>
> **Terms**: Pet rooms have 2 queen beds.
>
> **Pet Amenities**: There is plenty of space on property for walking pets.

Hampton Inn & Suites

725 South Lincoln Avenue 80487
970-871-8900 / 800-909-6285

> **Restaurant**: Within walking distance
>
> **H20**: Year round outdoor pool and three hot tubs
>
> **Pet Fee**: None
>
> **Refundable Pet Deposit**: None
>
> **Size Limit**: None
>
> **Terms**: Pets must be well-behaved.
>
> **Pet Amenities**: There is plenty of room on property for walking pets.

Holiday Inn Steamboat

3190 S. Lincoln Avenue 80477
970-879-2250 / 800-654-3944

> **Restaurant**: Village Inn
>
> **H20**: Year round outdoor pool and hot tub
>
> **Pet Fee**: $10 per night per pet
>
> **Refundable Pet Deposit**: $25
>
> **Size Limit**: None
>
> **Terms**: Pets cannot be left in room unattended.
>
> **Pet Amenities**: A doggie cookie upon arrival. Plenty of grass for you to walk your pets.
>
> **Fido's Favorite Features**: Nice pool area. The hotel is conveniently located near the Yampa Cove trail walking path. Pet-friendly staff.

Iron Horse Inn - Steamboat Springs
333 South Lincoln Avenue 80477
970-879-6505 / 800-856-6505

Restaurant: Several within walking distance

H20: Outdoor hot tub

Pet Fee: $15 per stay per room

Refundable Pet Deposit: None

Size Limit: None

Terms: Well-behaved pets welcome.

Pet Amenities: There are grassy areas nearby for walking pets.

"To err is human, to forgive, canine."

-Unknown

Rabbit Ears Motel
201 Lincoln Avenue 80477
970-879-1150 / 800-828-7702

> **Restaurant**: Walking distance
>
> **H20**: Discounted passes to hot springs pool across the street.
>
> **Pet Fee**: $12 per stay per pet
>
> **Refundable Pet Deposit**: None
>
> **Size Limit**: None
>
> **Terms**: Pets cannot be left unattended in rooms.
>
> **Pet Amenities**: Yampa River Park and the river itself are conveniently located next to the property. There is plenty of space for Fido to exercise on property. Pet pick up supplies are available at the front desk.

Sheraton Steamboat Resort
2200 Village Inn Court 80487
970-879-2220 / 800-848-8877

> **Restaurant**: Seven's, Three Saddles Lounge
>
> **H20**: Year round outdoor pool and six hot tubs
>
> **Pet Fee**: $25 per stay per room
>
> **Refundable Pet Deposit**: None
>
> **Size Limit**: 80 lbs.
>
> **Terms**: Pets cannot be left unattended in rooms.
>
> **Pet Amenities**: Signature Sheraton pet beds, pet welcome bags, pet dishes.
>
> **Fido's Favorite Features**: Great location! Deluxe accommodations, pool area, pet-friendly staff! This is a fantastic property located at the base of the ski area.

Super 8 Motel
3195 South Lincoln Avenue 80487
970-879-5230 / 800-800-8000

> **Restaurant**: Within walking distance.
>
> **H20**: Seasonal outdoor pool, outdoor hot tub
>
> **Pet Fee**: None
>
> **Refundable Pet Deposit**: $20
>
> **Size Limit**: None
>
> **Terms:** Pets cannot be left unattended in room.
>
> **Pet Amenities**: There are areas to walk your pets on property.

-Sterling-

Best Western Sundowner
125 Overland Trail 80751
970-522-6265 / 800-WESTERN

Restaurant: Short drive

H20: Indoor hot tub, seasonal outdoor pool

Pet Fee: $10 per night per pet

Refundable Pet Deposit: None

Size Limit: None

Terms: Must be in a smoking room.

Pet Amenities: There is an open field behind the property for walking your pets.

Ramada Inn Sterling
22140 East Highway 6 80751
970-522-2625 / 800-835-7275

Restaurant: Country Kitchen

H20: Indoor pool and hot tub

Pet Fee: None

Refundable Pet Deposit: $25 cash or credit card

Size Limit: None

Terms: Pet rooms have an exterior entrance.

Pet Amenities: There is a grassy area behind the property to walk your pets.

-Stratton-

Best Western Golden Prairie Inn
700 Colorado Avenue 80836
719-348-5311 / 800-626-0043

Restaurant: The Golden Prairie Inn

H20: Seasonal outdoor pool and hot tub

Pet Fee: None

Refundable Pet Deposit: None

Size Limit: None

Terms: Must declare pets at check in. Well-behaved pets only.

Pet Amenities: A designated pet relief area is located on property.

-Telluride-

The Camel's Garden Resort Hotel

250 West San Juan 81435

970-728-9300 / 888-772-2635

Restaurant: Chair 8

H20: Large outdoor hot tub

Pet Fee: $40 per night per room

Refundable Pet Deposit: None

Size Limit: None

Terms: Must sign pet agreement at check in.

Pet Amenities: Rooms on ground floor with door opening out to Gondola Plaza and the river trail for nice pet walks.

Fido's Favorite Features: Spacious and plush accommodations, wonderful beds, ideal location, great hot tub, accommodating staff. This impressive hotel offers a nice complimentary expanded breakfast and afternoon social hour. The pet friendly gondola connects the town of Telluride to the Mountain Village.

*Be sure to walk your pooch down to Mountain Tails pet supply store for all of Fido's needs.

The Wyndham Peaks Resort & Golden Door Spa

136 Country Club Drive 81435

970-728-6800 / 800-789-2220

Restaurant: The Navarra, Legends, The Great Room

H20: Indoor / outdoor pool, three indoor hot tubs, two outdoor hot tubs

Pet Fee: $100 per

Refundable Pet Deposit: None

Size Limit: None

Terms: Guest is responsible for pet's behavior.

Pet Amenities: Bowls, treats, bones and beds provided. There is plenty of room to walk your dog on property.

Fido's Favorite Features: The Golden Door Spa, gorgeous views, excellent bath products, great location, luxurious doggie spa. You don't even need to leave the resort, The Wyndham Peaks truly has it all!

The Doggie Spa at the Wyndham Peaks Resort & Golden Door® Spa is the perfect Telluride destination for travelers who can't bear to leave Fido behind. The program promotes a healthy lifestyle for dogs of any shape and size.

Doggie guests are treated to V.I.P. service upon arrival where they receive a welcome kit and dog-friendly in-room amenities. During their stay, pooches are pampered with an array of dog-friendly activities outdoors and in the Golden Door Spa, including guided playtime and 25-minute doggie massages, a service that can also be enjoyed in-room.

For additional information or to book a Doggie Spa package at the Wyndham Peaks, please call (800) WYNDHAM or visit www.wyndham.com.

-Thornton-

Sleep Inn North Denver

12101 Grant Street 80233

303-280-9818 / 800-424-6423

Restaurant: Several within walking distance.

H20: Indoor pool and hot tub

Pet Fee: $5 per night per pet

Refundable Pet Deposit: None

Size Limit: None

Terms: Two dogs per room maximum.

Pet Amenities: There is plenty of grass on property for walking pets.

-Trinidad-

Best Western Trinidad Inn
900 W. Adams Street 81082
719-846-2215 / 800-955-2215

Restaurant: The Family Seed II

H20: Indoor hot tub, seasonal outdoor pool

Pet Fee: None

Refundable Pet Deposit: None

Size Limit: None

Terms: Dogs and cats are both welcome. Pets cannot be left unattended in room.

Pet Amenities: There is ample space to walk your dog on the property.

Budget Summit Inn
9800 Santa Fe Trail Drive 81082
719-846-2251

Restaurant: Within walking distance.

H20: None

Pet Fee: $10 per night per room

Refundable Pet Deposit: None

Size Limit: None

Terms: Pets must be well-behaved.

Pet Amenities: Plenty of grass on property for walking pets.

Quality Inn Trinidad
3125 Toupal Drive 81082
719-846-4491 / 800-4CHOICE

Restaurant: Country Kitchen

H20: Indoor pool and hot tub

Pet Fee: $15 per night per pet

Refundable Pet Deposit: None

Size Limit: None

Terms: Pets cannot be left unattended in room.

Pet Amenities: Plenty of space to walk pets on property.

Super 8 Motel

1924 Freedom Road 81082
719-846-8280 / 800-800-8000

Restaurant: Walking distance

H20: None

Pet Fee: $10 per room per stay

Refundable Pet Deposit: None

Size Limit: None

Terms: Pets cannot be left unattended in room.

Pet Amenities: There is a large empty field behind the property for walking pets.

-Vail-

Antler's at Vail

680 West Lionshead Place 81657
970-476-2471 / 800-843-8245

Restaurant: Walking distance

H20: Outdoor pool and two hot tubs

Pet Fee: $15 per day per pet

Refundable Pet Deposit: None

Size Limit: "We've had Mumbles stay with us. He's a 232 pound mastiff. That's the limit."

Terms: Quiet and friendly pets only, please.

Pet Amenities: Welcome bags for pets at check in. Pet waste bags available at front desk. There is plenty of room to walk your pets on property.

Holiday Inn

2211 N. Frontage Rd. 81657
970-476-3890 / 800-HOLIDAY

Restaurant: Bagalis, Sushi Nogewe, West Side Cafe

H20: Outdoor pool, indoor hot tub

Pet Fee: $25 per night per pet

Refundable Pet Deposit: None

Size Limit: None

Terms: Two pets per room maximum. Pets cannot be left unattended in room.

Pet Amenities: There is a vacant four-acre lot to exercise your pets.

Lifthouse Condos

5555 E. Lionshead Circle 81657

970-476-2340 / 800-654-0635

Restaurant: Bart & Yeti's, Montauk's Seafood Grille

H20: Indoor hot tub

Pet Fee: $25 per night per room

Refundable Pet Deposit: None

Size Limit: None

Terms: Pets cannot be left unattended in room at any time. Must sign pet policy agreement at check in.

Pet Amenities: Treats are available at the front desk. There is plenty of space to walk pets on property.

Vail Cascade Resort & Spa
1300 Westhaven Drive 81657
970-476-7111 / 800-303-7954

Restaurant: Chap's Grill & Chop House, Blue Tiger

H20: Two year round outdoor pools and 3 hot tubs.

Pet Fee: $25 per day per pet. Subject to change, please call in advance.

Refundable Pet Deposit: None

Size Limit: None

Terms: Well-behaved pets welcome. Two pets maximum. Pets must be leashed in public areas. Pets must be crated if left in room unattended. Owner is responsible for pet's behavior.

Pet Amenities: Pet beds, bowls and daily treats included in pet fee. Gore Creek Trail located behind hotel for walking Fido. Most pet rooms are ground level with a private patio.

Fido's Favorite Features: Chap's Grill & Chop House, Aria Spa & Club, ideal ski-in/ski-out location. A great destination vacation spot during both winter and summer.

-Walsenburg-

Best Western Rambler
457 U.S. Highway 85-87 81089
719-738-1121 / 866-224-7016

Restaurant: The Rambler

H20: Seasonal outdoor pool

Pet Fee: None

Refundable Pet Deposit: None

Size Limit: None

Terms: Must be in a smoking room.

Pet Amenities: There is a dog walking area on property.

Make sure your pet is current on all required vaccinations. While on the road, carry proof from your Veterinarian.

-Westminster-

Doubletree Hotel - Denver North
8773 Yates Drive 80030
303-427-4000 / 800-222-TREE

> **Restaurant**: Lafittes
>
> **H20**: Indoor pool and hot tub
>
> **Pet Fee**: None
>
> **Refundable Pet Deposit**: $50
>
> **Size Limit**: 50 lbs.
>
> **Terms**: Pets cannot be left unattended in room at any time.
>
> **Pet Amenities**: There are grassy areas on property to walk your pets.
>
> **Fido's Favorite Features**: Lafittes, comfortable accommodations, pet-friendly staff.

La Quinta Inn & Suites Westminster
10179 Church Ranch Way 80021
303-438-5800 / 800-531-5900

> **Restaurant**: Short drive
>
> **H20**: Indoor pool and hot tub
>
> **Pet Fee**: None
>
> **Refundable Pet Deposit**: $50 cash or credit card
>
> **Size Limit**: None
>
> **Terms**: Guest is responsible for damage caused by pets.
>
> **Pet Amenities**: Well trained, quiet pets only. There is an ample dog walking area on property.

La Quinta Inn Westminster Mall
8701 Turnpike Drive 80030
303-425-9099 / 800-531-5900

> **Restaurant**: Walking distance
>
> **H20**: Seasonal outdoor pool
>
> **Pet Fee**: None
>
> **Refundable Pet Deposit**: None
>
> **Size Limit**: None
>
> **Terms**: Well-behaved pets only.
>
> **Pet Amenities**: There are grassy areas on property for walking dogs.

Traveling With Your Pet ...In Style!

The Westin Westminster

10600 Westminster Boulevard 80020
303-410-5000 / 800-WESTIN1

Restaurant: O's

H20: Indoor pool, outdoor hot tub

Pet Fee: None

Refundable Pet Deposit: None

Size Limit: None

Terms: Pets cannot be left unattended in room. Well-behaved pets welcome.

Pet Amenities: There are plenty of areas around the property to walk your pets. There are walking trails nearby. Pet beds provided.

Fido's Favorite Features: The spacious and plush accommodations, the heavenly beds, O's. This stylish hotel is a short walk from several entertainment and dining options.

Westminster Super 8

12055 Melody Drive 80234
303-451-7200 / 800-800-8000

Restaurant: Walking distance

H20: Indoor hot tub

Pet Fee: $5 per night per pet

Refundable Pet Deposit: None

Size Limit: None

Terms: Pets cannot be left unattended in room.

Pet Amenities: There is ample space on property for walking pets.

-Wheat Ridge-

Ramada Inn

4700 Kipling Street 80033
303-423-4000 / 800-2RAMADA

Restaurant: Walking distance

H20: Seasonal outdoor pool

Pet Fee: $25 per stay per pet

Refundable Pet Deposit: None

Size Limit: None

Terms: Pets cannot be left unattended in room.

Pet Amenities: There is a grassy area on property and an open field to walk your dog.

-Windsor-

Americinn Lodge & Suites
7645 Westgate Drive 80528
970-226-1232 / 800-634-3444

> **Restaurant**: Several within walking distance
>
> **H20**: Indoor pool and hot tub
>
> **Pet Fee**: $10 per night per pet
>
> **Refundable Pet Deposit**: None
>
> **Size Limit**: None
>
> **Terms**: There are only a few pet rooms. Best to call in advance for reservation.
>
> **Pet Amenities**: There is plenty of room to walk your pets on property.

Super 8 Motel
1265 Main Street 80550
970-686-5996

> **Restaurant**: Several within walking distance.
>
> **H20**: Outdoor hot tub
>
> **Pet Fee**: $15 per night per pet
>
> **Refundable Pet Deposit**: None
>
> **Size Limit**: None
>
> **Terms**: Well-behaved pets only.
>
> **Pet Amenities**: Large, grassy area behind property for walking pets.

-Winter Park-

Beaver Village Lodge
79303 U.S. Highway 40 80482
970-726-5741 / 800-666-0281

> **Restaurant**: Walking distance
>
> **H20**: Two indoor hot tubs
>
> **Pet Fee**: None
>
> **Refundable Pet Deposit**: None
>
> **Size Limit**: None
>
> **Terms**: Well-behaved pets are welcome.
>
> **Pet Amenities**: There is plenty of room to walk your pets on property.

The Vintage Hotel Resort 🐾 🐾 🐾 🐾 🐾

100 Winter Park Drive 80482

970-726-8801 / 800-472-7017

Restaurant: Tipper's Tavern

H20: Outdoor pool and hot tub

Pet Fee: $25 per room per stay

Refundable Pet Deposit: None

Size Limit: None

Terms: Guest is responsible for damages caused by pets.

Pet Amenities: Dog biscuits at check in. Plenty of room for pets to run on property. Tipper, the house dog, will greet you and your pet.

Fido's Favorite Features: Ideal ski location, nice pool area, extremely pet friendly hotel. The Vintage Hotel is a great destination for skiers who want to bring their pets along. A swim in the inviting pool is the perfect way to wind down at the end of the day.

Winter Park Mountain Lodge 🐾 🐾 🐾

81699 U.S. Highway 40 80482

970-726-4211 / 800-726-3340

Restaurant: The Moffat Station Restaurant & Brewery

H20: Indoor pool and two hot tubs

Pet Fee: None

Refundable Pet Deposit: None

Size Limit: None

Terms: Must declare pets at check in. Designated pet rooms. Guest is responsible for damage caused by pets.

Pet Amenities: Ample walking areas on property. Hiking trails located behind the hotel.

Traveling With Your Pet ...In Style!

-Woodland Park-

Pikes Peak Paradise B&B
236 Pinecrest Rd. 80863
719-687-6656 / 800-728-8282

Restaurant: Short drive

H20: Outdoor hot tub

Pet Fee: $10 per day per pet

Refundable Pet Deposit: $100

Size Limit: None

Terms: There is only one pet room, a deluxe suite with private entrance. Call in advance.

Pet Amenities: The property is located in a nice neighborhood for walking pets.

-Yampa-

Oak Tree Inn
98 Moffat Avenue 80483
970-638-1000

Restaurant: Penny's Diner

H20: Indoor hot tub

Pet Fee: $10 per room per stay

Refundable Pet Deposit: None

Size Limit: None

Terms: Well-behaved pets welcome.

Pet Amenities: Plenty of room on property for walking pets.

Some pets have sensitive stomachs, so it can be a good idea to bring their familiar water from home.

FIDO'S FINEST TOP PICKS
FOR A DESTINATION VACATION

Downhill Skiing

The Ritz-Carlton Bachelor Gulch - Beaver Creek

The Sky Hotel - Aspen

Silvertree Hotel - Snowmass

Grand Lodge - Crested Butte

Sheraton Hotel - Steamboat

The Great Divide Lodge - Breckenridge

Vintage Hotel - Winter Park

The Wyndham Peaks Resort - Telluride

Rochester Hotel - Durango

Vail Cascade Resort & Spa - Vail

Golf - Stay & Play

Omni Interlocken-
Omni Interlocken Golf Club, Broomfield

Doubletree Hotel-
Redlands Mesa Golf Club, Grand Junction

Purple Mountain Lodge-
Crested Butte Country Club, Crested Butte

Westin Tabor Center-
The Ridge at Castle Pines North, Castle Rock

Quality Inn & Suites-
The Raven Golf Club at Three Peaks, Silverthorne

TownePlace Suites-
Arrowhead Golf Club, Littleton

Westin Westminster-
Vista Ridge Golf Club, Erie

Ridgway/Ouray Lodge & Suites-
Fairway Pines Golf Club, Ridgway

The Inn at Keystone-
The River Course at Keystone, Keystone

Sheraton Hotel-
Sheraton Steamboat Golf Club, Steamboat Springs

The Vintage Hotel-
Pole Creek Golf Club, Winter Park

Embassy Suites Hotel-
Green Valley Ranch, Aurora (near DIA)

Sheraton Hotel, Denver Tech Center-
The Golf Club at Bear Dance, Larkspur

Rochester Hotel-
Dalton Ranch Golf Club, Durango

Ritz-Carlton Bachelor Gulch-
Red Sky Golf Club, Wolcott

Hiking / Biking / Cross Country Skiing

The Ruby of Crested Butte B&B - Crested Butte
Hotel Lenado - Aspen
The Vintage Hotel - Winter Park
Sheraton Hotel - Steamboat Springs
The Ritz-Carlton Bachelor Gulch - Avon

Hot Springs

The Springs Resort - Pagosa Springs
Hotel Colorado - Glenwood Springs
Ouray Victorian Inn - Ouray
Rabbit Ears Motel - Steamboat Springs
Ridgway Lodge & Suites - Ridgway

Rafting

Travelodge - Salida
Best Western Royal Gorge Motel - Canon City
Three Rivers Resort - Almont
Best Western Vista Inn - Buena Vista
Hotel Denver - Glenwood Springs

Retail Therapy

Hotel Jerome - Downtown Aspen
JW Marriott - Cherry Creek Mall, Denver
Omni Interlocken - Flatiron Crossing Mall, Broomfield
Denver West Marriott - Colorado Mills, Golden
Staybridge Suites - Park Meadows Mall, Lone Tree
Best Western Inn & Suites - Castle Rock Outlet Mall
Camel's Garden Hotel - Downtown Telluride
Westin Tabor Center - Sixteenth Street Mall, Denver
Quality Inn & Suites - Silverthorne Outlet Mall
Marriott Hotel - Foothills Mall, Fort Collins

Spa Retreats

The Ritz Carlton Bachelor Gulch- The Ritz-Carlton Spa- Avon
The Wyndham Peaks Resort - The Golden Door Spa- Telluride
St. Regis Hotel - Remede Spa- Aspen
The Hotel Monaco - The Renaissance Aveda Spa- Denver
The Omni Interlocken Resort - The Omni Spa- Broomfield
Purple Mountain B& B - An Essential Escape- Crested Butte
Camel's Garden Hotel - Atmosphere Spa- Telluride
The Springs Resort - Healing Waters- Pagosa Springs
Chipeta Sun Lodge & Spa - Ridgway
Vail Cascade Resort & Spa - Aria Spa & Club- Vail

Stay & Dine Fine

Hotel Teatro - Denver
JW Marriott - Denver
Omni Interlocken - Broomfield
Ritz-Carlton Bachelor Gulch - Avon
The Little Nell - Aspen
The Hotel Monaco - Denver
St. Regis - Aspen
Westin Hotel - Westminster
The Wyndham Peaks Resort - Telluride
Westin Tabor Center - Denver

Stay & Lounge by the Pool

The Ritz-Carlton Bachelor Gulch - Avon
The Wyndham Peaks Resort - Telluride
The Sky Hotel - Aspen
The Omni Interlocken Resort - Broomfield
The Vintage Hotel - Winter Park
The Grand Lodge - Crested Butte
Sheraton Hotel - Steamboat Springs
Westin Tabor Center - Denver
The Antlers at Vail - Vail
Silvertree Hotel - Snowmass

Weekend in Denver

The Hotel Teatro
JW Marriott
Hotel Monaco
Westin Tabor Center
Loews Denver Hotel

Dog-Friendly Parks & Off-Leash Areas that we discovered.

(Not all parks are leash-free, but do allow pets)

Aspen:
Wagner Park
Located along Monarch Street downtown Aspen.

Aurora:
Cherry Creek State Park
Located at Parker & Orchard.
Grandview Off-Leash Dog Park
Located on Quincy Avenue, just west of the Quincy Reservoir.

Boulder:

East Boulder Dog Park
Located on 55th Street, just south of South Boulder Road.

Howard Heuston Park & Off-Leash Area
Located on 34th Street, east of Iris Avenue.

Valmont Dog Park
Located on Valmont Road between Airport Road and 55th Street.

Breckenridge:

Carter Park
Located at the south end of High Street.

Colorado Springs:

Bear Creek Off-Leash Area
Located at the northern end of the park, on East 21st Street.

Palmer Park Dog Park
Located off Maizeland near Academy, north of Constitution.

Rampart Dog Park
Located on Lexington Drive, just north of Lexington & N. Union.

Denver:

Barnum Park
Located at Hooker Street & West 5th Avenue.

Berkeley Park
Located at Sheridan Avenue & West 46th Street.

Denver Off-Leash Dog Park
Located on South Jason Street, behind the Denver Animal
Control Building.

Fuller Park Located at Franklin Street & East 29th Avenue.

Green Valley Ranch East Park
Located at Jebel & East 45th.

Kennedy Park
Located at Hampden Avenue & South Dayton Street.

Montview Dog Park
Located in Stapleton Development on Syracuse, just north of
Syracuse & Montview.

Washington Park
Streets bordering this huge park are Downing Street, Louisiana
Avenue, Franklin Street and Virginia Avenue.

Durango:

Durango Dog Park / Off-Leash Area
Located at Smelter Mountain & Highway 160 West.

Englewood:

Centennial Park Off-Leash Area
Located on Union Street between Santa Fe & Federal.
Northwest Greenbelt
Located on Tejon, just north of Dartmouth & Tejon.

Estes Park:

Estes Park Dog Park
Located off US 36, east of the Stanley Park Fairgrounds.

Evergreen:
Bark Park Off-Leash Area
Located on Stagecoach Road just past the Elk Meadows sign.

Fort Collins:
Fossil Creek Dog Park
Located on Lemay just south of Harmony & Lemay.
Spring Canyon Park
Located on the west end of Horsetooth Road.

Glenwood Springs:
Glenwood Springs Dog Park
Located along the river and can be accessed by the South Grand Trail.

Golden:
Dog Park at Tony Grampsas
Located at West 44th Avenue & Salvia Street.

Greeley:

Rover's Run Dog Park
Located west of downtown, on F Street, near 59th Avenue.

Highlands Ranch:

Rover's Run at Redstone Park
Located at Foothills Canyon Blvd. & Town Center Drive.

Littleton:

Bark Park
Located on East County Line Road between Holly & Colorado Blvd.

Chatfield State Park Off-Leash Area
Located at Wadsworth and C-470.

Highland Heritage Dog Park
Located at University & Quebec.

Longmont:

Longmont Airport Dog Park
Located on St. Vrain Road, just north of the airport.

Longmont Francis Dog Park
Located at Francis and 21st.

Northglenn:

Happy Tails Dog Park
Located near 106th Avenue and Irma Drive.

Steamboat Springs:

Dr. Rich Weiss Park
Located on Hwy 40 across from the hot springs swimming pool.

Telluride:

Telluride Town Park
Located east of downtown on Colorado Avenue.

Westminster:

Westminster Open Space Off-Leash Dog Park
Located between 103rd and 108th on the west side of Simms Street.